3rd Edition

Perfect
800
SAT Math

Perfect

3rd Edition

Advanced Strategies for Top Students

800
SAT Math

Dan Celenti, Ph.D.

Prufrock Press Inc.
Waco, Texas

Library of Congress Cataloging-in-Publication Data

Names: Celenti, Dan, 1952- | Compton, Lacy, editor.
Title: Perfect 800 : SAT math : advanced strategies for top students / by Dan Celenti, Ph.D.
Other titles: Perfect eight hundred | SAT math
Description: Third edition. | Waco, Texas : Prufrock Press, Inc., [2017] |
  "Edited by Lacy Compton."
Identifiers: LCCN 2016058266 | ISBN 9781618216229 (pbk.)
Subjects: LCSH: Mathematics--Examinations--Study guides. | SAT (Educational
  test)--Study guides.
Classification: LCC QA43 .C34 2017 | DDC 510.76--dc23
LC record available at https://lccn.loc.gov/2016058266

Printed in the United States of America.

At the time of this book's publication, all facts and figures cited are the most current available. All telephone numbers, addresses, and website URLs are accurate and active. All publications, organizations, websites, and other resources exist as described in the book, and all have been verified. The author and Prufrock Press Inc. make no warranty or guarantee concerning the information and materials given out by organizations or content found at websites, and we are not responsible for any changes that occur after this book's publication. If you find an error, please contact Prufrock Press Inc.

Prufrock Press Inc.
P. O. Box 8813
Waco, TX 76714-8813
Phone: (800) 998-2208
Fax: (800) 240-0333
http://www.prufrock.com

The value of an education . . . is not the learning of many facts
but the training of the mind to think.

—Albert Einstein

Contents

Chapter 6: Trigonometry 147

Chapter 7: Miscellaneous Topics 153

Chapter 8: Problems by Degree of Difficulty and Type 163

Acknowledgements

To the students I had the privilege to work with over the years, I am extremely grateful. I want to thank them for putting up with my occasionally unconventional methods of teaching math, providing me with candid and useful feedback, and—most of all—for making my interaction with them translate into hours of fun and rewarding work.

In addition, I want to thank my children for fueling my passion for smart education; Dr. MAC (Jean D'Arcy Maculaitis, Ph.D., President and founder of MAC Testing & Consulting, LLC) for being the catalyst for my involvement in various aspects of SAT preparation and—through her work and dedication of many years—providing me with a continuous source of inspiration; and my wife for her relentless support and encouragement.

Foreword to the Third Edition

Given the tremendous number of SAT books on the market, the reception received by the first (2010) and the updated (2014) editions of this book far exceeded my expectations. The fact that so many parents, students, and even educational organizations[1] embraced the idea that math should not be a continuous exercise in memorization and applying trial-end-error using a calculator, but rather a quest to improve one's analytic/critical thinking skills, was extremely encouraging and certainly played a major role in the decision to work on a new edition. This new edition, of course, was created to take into account the major changes that the College Board implemented in its "New" SAT since March 16, 2016.

When it comes to the need to update and publish a new edition of a test preparatory book like this, the author is always challenged to strike the right balance between novelty and material that can be reused. (After all, as a colleague of mine jokingly put it, "the Pythagorean Theorem hasn't really changed much since the publication of the previous edition!")

To provide some insight into the driving force behind and the "novelty" of this edition, the changes made by the College Board (in content and format) were summarized in Table 1 with additional specifics on the changes implemented starting March 2016 illustrated in Table 2.

Finally, in case you missed this, here is the good news for all of you math enthusiasts: The math score in the new SAT *accounts for half of the total score*!

As always, I look forward to your comments, questions, and suggestions.

Dan Celenti
dan.celenti@gmail.com
July 2016

---

1   The National Organization for Gifted and Talented Students used the updated edition of this book as a textbook for its SAT courses offered in its Summer Institute for the Gifted (SIG) camps in 2014 and 2015.

TABLE 1
"Old" Versus "New" SAT

Category	"Old" SAT	"New" SAT
Total Time	3 hours 45 minutes (25-minute essay is mandatory)	3 hours 50 minutes (50-minute essay is optional)

Components/ Time/Number of Questions	• Critical Reading/50 minutes/67
	• Writing/60 minutes/49
	• Math/70 minutes/54
	• Essay (mandatory)/25 minutes/1
		• Evidence-Based Reading and Writing
		  ⊙ Reading Test/65 minutes/52
		  ⊙ Writing and Language/35 minutes/44
		  ⊙ Math (78%/22%; mc/oe)
		    » No-calculators/25 minutes/20 (15/5; mc/oe)
		    » Calculators/55 minutes/38 (30/8; mc/oe)
		  ⊙ Essay (optional)/50 minutes/1

Philosophy	• Emphasis on general reasoning skills and vocabulary • Penalties for incorrect answers • Essay (mandatory) given at the beginning of the test; students are required to take a position on a presented issue	• Stronger emphasis on reasoning and stronger focus on knowledge skills deemed important for college success and career readiness • Greater emphasis on the meaning of the words in extended context and how word choice shapes the meaning, tone, and impact • No penalties for wrong answers • Essay (optional) given at the end of the SAT; students are required to analyze a provided source text
Score	• Composite Score: (600–2400) • Area Scores: 3 (200–800; Critical Reading, Writing, and Math) • Test Scores: N/A • Cross-Test Scores: N/A • Subscores: N/A • Essay: Combined scores of two raters each scoring on a 1–6 scale	• Composite Score: 400–1600 • Area Scores: 2 (200–800; Evidence-Based Reading and Writing + Math) • Test Scores: 3 (10–40; Reading, Writing and Language, Math) • Cross-Test Scores: 2 (10–40; Analysis in Science and History/Social Studies; based on selected questions from the two main areas) • Subscores: 7 (1–15; Command of Evidence, Relevant Words in Context, Expression of Ideas, Standard English Conventions, Heart of Algebra, Problem Solving and Data Analysis, Passport to Advance Math) • Essay: Combined scores of two raters, each scoring on a 1–4 scale

Note. mc/oe = multiple choice/open-ended.

TABLE 2

The "New" SAT

When	Started spring (March) 2016
Format	Print or (in selected locations) computer based
Content	• Evidence-Based Reading and Writing (Section 1: Reading Test; Section 2: Writing and Language Test) • Math (Section 3: Math—No Calculators; Section 4: Math—Calculators) • Optional essay
Scoring	Total score range: 400–1600 (200–800 combined score for Sections 1 and 2, 3 and 4, respectively); the score for the essay will be reported separately
Time	3 hours, plus 50 minutes for the optional essay
What's Really New (General)?	• Score: Max 1600 (instead of 2400) • Essay: Optional (at the end not at the beginning) • Philosophy/goal—College Board: Aligned more closely with what students study in high school and will confront in college and predict college academic performance more accurately and fairly while resisting short-term coaching (**Q:** How? **A:** Via questions more grounded in the "real world") • Philosophy/goal—Pragmatic view: Making the SAT look more like the ACT; an effort seems to be made to emphasize analytic/critical thinking skills (**Q:** How? **A:** By answering questions that require an ability to interpret data/info, synthesize, look for and use evidence to explain arguments/points of view, taking a multistep approach to problem solving—all in a context that would better emulate the "real world")
What's Really New (Specific)?	• Evidence-Based Reading and Writing ⊙ Vocabulary: Focus on relevant words (eliminating the need to memorize rarely used/obscure words) ⊙ Emphasize writing skills and require good command of evidence ⊙ To emphasize the importance of citizenship (in addition to college/career), tests will include excerpts from one of the founding documents (*Declaration of Independence, Constitution, Bill of Rights*) or ongoing Great Global Conversation (topics such as freedom, human rights/dignity, justice) ⊙ The (optional) essay: Instead of a time-limited writing sample, students will read a passage and have to explain (based on evidence) the author's point of view/argument(s) • Math ⊙ No penalty for wrong answers ⊙ The multiple-choice problems will have four (instead of five) choices ⊙ Will include more multistep problems ⊙ Problems will be less abstract and have a more real-life context ⊙ Focus on three areas: *problem solving and data analysis* (achieving quantitative literacy; i.e., solve "real-life" problems using ratios, percentages, and proportional reasoning), *algebra* (linear equations and systems), and *"advanced" math* (solving "more complex" equations)

Introduction:
Why Another SAT Book

The real voyage of discovery consists not in seeking
new landscapes but in having new eyes.

—Marcel Proust

The vast majority of SAT-prep books are structured as "one-size-fits-all" products. As a result, (a) students struggling in math find themselves emerged into a system that does not provide them with an easy strategy to improve (i.e., that would allow them to identify and work on their weaknesses) and (b) advanced students would find a significant percentage of the covered topics and—in general—content to be too easy and thus of insignificant—if any—value to them.

This book is designed to primarily address the needs of gifted and advanced students (i.e., students expected to score above 600 on the math section of the SAT, as shown in Figures 1 and 2) by showcasing various math topics via problems which level of difficulty is (mostly) above average. In addition, it offers an approach to studying that emphasizes the importance of logical thinking and the idea of reasoning as paramount to problem solving.

This book's methodology not only will ensure that every topic is well-suited for its audience of gifted and advanced students but also, by emphasizing critical thinking/analytic skills, will result in a much more optimal usage of students' time and maximize the pace of progress in preparing for the test.

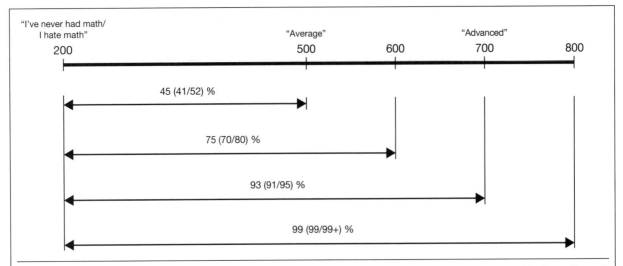

Figure 1. Graphic representation of SAT Percentile Ranks for 2015 college-bound seniors (College Board, 2015). *Note.* Total = male + female students.

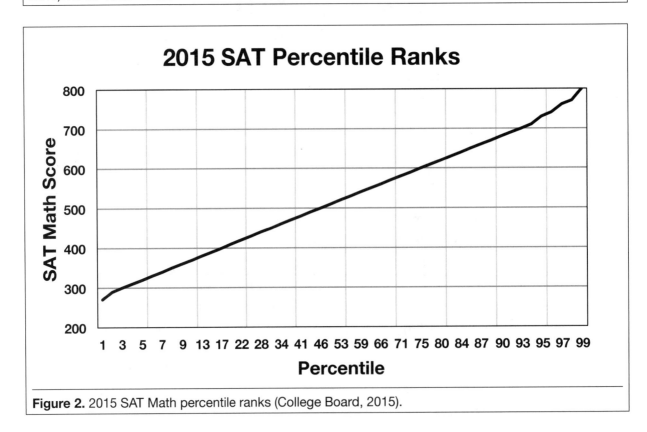

Figure 2. 2015 SAT Math percentile ranks (College Board, 2015).

This Book's Approach

The world we have created today ... has problems which cannot be
solved by thinking the way we thought when we created them.

—Albert Einstein

Although compared to the rest of the test, the math (Sections 3 and 4 in
the new test) portion has arguably changed the least, there still are significant changes (in format and content) that this new edition intends to address.

An essential novelty of the new test consists in the fact that the math
score contributes half of the total score (as opposed to one-third in the "old"
SAT format.) There is greater emphasis on *data interpretation and graphs*,
analyzing and solving equations, and the need to test math skills in the context of *more realistic scenarios*. As a result, good reading comprehension skills
play an increased role as students should expect more multiple-step problems
and be aware of the fact that in one of the two math sections (Section 3) calculators are not allowed.

A couple of notable content changes in the new test are a *decreased emphasis on geometry* and the addition of *new topics such as elements of trigonometry
and complex numbers*. In addition, students are *no longer penalized for wrong
answers* in multiple-choice problems for which they now have *four (instead of
five) options* to choose from.

A summary of logistics the author took into account in his approach to helping students prepare and exceed in the math sections of the new SAT are illustrated in Tables 3 and 4.

Table 5 summarizes math topics/concepts that will be covered throughout the book.

Finally, an explanation of the scoring methodology is summarized in Table 6.

Scattered throughout the book are more than 235 problems solved as "test cases." They were selected for (a) being representative for an entire category of problems that historically were given in real tests and (b) their suitability for showcasing the importance of logic and analytic skills over memorization. In addition, 21 brain teasers/mind games are included to help students improve their reading comprehension and analytic/critical thinking skills. Access to a complete online test (58 problems) is also provided to assess students' readiness for the test by providing them with an in-depth analysis of their result/ scores.

Every time an example is given, students are strongly encouraged to take a few minutes not only to familiarize themselves with the problem but also to try to solve it. Only after that should they go over the solution suggested by the author. Note that almost without exception, the SAT math problems have unique solutions. Most often than not, depending on the complexity of the problem, the correct result can be obtained using more than one method/technique. Selecting and/or suggesting the "quickest" or the "smartest" method is a very subjective endeavor. It depends on a variety of personal traits and skill sets including, but not limited to, the prevalent memory type (e.g., visual or abstract), whether you are naturally inclined to rely more on logic or sheer memorization of factual knowledge or formulas, familiarity with algebraic techniques, knowledge breadth, and so forth. As a result, it is not the author's intention to suggest that his way of solving a problem is either (a) the only way or (b) the best way. It is, however, his intention to use his approach as a brainstorming exercise that would eventually act as a catalyst in helping students develop their own problem-solving approach and methodology.

This book includes an online test (see http://www.prufrock.com/perfect800) that, once completed, will generate an in-depth analysis of your results and a list of recommendations for an improved performance.

This book's philosophy and approach are eloquently summarized in the words of Albert Einstein:

"Any fool can know. The point is to understand."

TABLE 3

"New" SAT Math (1)

Category	"New" SAT
Time	Total: 80 minutes • No-Calculator (Section 3): 25 minutes • Calculator (Section 4): 55 minutes
Question Type/ Number/ Percentage	• Multiple Choice (four choices)/45/78% • Student-Produced Response (grid-in)/13/22% *Note.* A multipart, word problem in the Problem Solving and Data Analysis category may be given at the end of Section 4.
Question Content/ Number/ Percentage	• Heart of Algebra/19/33% ⊙ Analyzing and solving equations/systems of equations ⊙ Creating expressions, equations, and inequalities to represent relationships between quantities and solve problems; rearranging and interpreting formulas ⊙ Absolute value ⊙ Lines in coordinate plane • Problem Solving and Data Analysis/17/29% ⊙ Creating and analyzing relationships using ratios, proportions, units, and percentage ⊙ Describing relationships in graphical format ⊙ Summarizing qualitative and quantitative data (intro to statistics) • Passport to Advanced Math/16/28% • Rewriting expressions using their structure ⊙ Exponential functions and radicals ⊙ Creating, analyzing, and solving quadratic and higher order equations (algebraic vs. graphical representations of functions) ⊙ Manipulating polynomials to solve problems • Additional Topics in Math/6/10% ⊙ Making area and volume calculations in context ⊙ Investigating lines, angles, triangles, and circles using theorems ⊙ Working with trigonometric functions ⊙ Imaginary and complex numbers • Contribution of Items to Across-Test Scores ⊙ Analysis in Science/8/23% ⊙ Analysis in History/Social Studies/8/23%
New Format and Content (Topics)	• Multiple-choice problems have four instead of five options • For multiple-choice problems, no penalties applied to wrong answers • Trigonometric functions, complex numbers included

---

TABLE 4

"New" SAT Math (2)

Section Type	"New" SAT
No-Calculator Section 3: Question Type/Number/ Percentage	Type (100%): • Multiple Choice/15/75% • Student-Produced Responses/5/25% Content (100%): • Heart of Algebra/8/40% • Passport to Advanced Math/9/45% • Additional Topics in Math/3/15% Total time: 25 minutes Total questions: 20 Total points: 20 (raw score)
Calculator Section 4: Question Type or Content/ Number/Percentage	Type (100%): • Multiple Choice/30/79% • Student-Produced Responses/8/21% Content (100%): • Heart of Algebra/11/29% • Problem Solving and Data Analysis/17/45% • Passport to Advanced Math/7/18% • Additional Topics in Math/3/8% Total time: 55 minutes Total questions: 38 Total points: 38 (raw score)

TABLE 5

Math Topics

Content/Topic	"New" SAT
Arithmetic	• Basic arithmetic concepts (including real numbers, integers, even/odd, absolute value, prime numbers, reciprocal numbers, least common multiple, greatest common factor/divisor, operations, quotient, remainder, order of operations, factors and factorization, sets, union, intersection, exponents, roots and square roots) • Fractions and decimals • Percents • Ratios and proportions • Averages (including weighted averages)
Algebra	• Polynomials (multiplication: distribution/FOIL method, factorization, binomials, etc.) • Solving equations and inequalities (including quadratic formula, solving sets of equations via substitution or elimination method) • Word problems (translation of English into Algebra)
Geometry	• Lines and angles • Triangles • Quadrilaterals and other polygons • Circles • Solid geometry • Coordinate geometry
Data Analysis	• Interpretation of data (including line and bar graphs, pie charts, and scatter plots)
Miscellaneous	• Counting and probability (including combinations and permutations, Venn diagrams, probabilities and compound probabilities) • Sequences (arithmetic and geometric) • Functions and their graphs • Trigonometry • Imaginary and complex numbers

TABLE 6

Math Scoring

Category	"New" SAT
Total Score (200–800)	Conversion Table (one-to-one): | Raw score	Total score | |---|---| | 1–58 | 200–800 |
Subscores (1–15) *Note.* Approximately 10 grid-in problems.	• Heart of Algebra (33%) (Max raw score = 19) ⊙ Math Test—No Calculator: 8 ⊙ Math Test—Calculator: 11 • Problem Solving and Data Analysis (29%) (Max raw score = 17) ⊙ Math Test—No Calculator: 0 ⊙ Math Test—Calculator: 17 • Passport to Advanced Math (28%) (Max raw score = 16) ⊙ Math Test—No Calculator: 9 ⊙ Math Test—Calculator: 7 Conversion Table: | Raw score	Subscores | |---|---| | 1–16/17/19 | 1–15 |
Cross-Test Scores (10–40) Stats: 8 out of 35 = 23% of total score No calculator = 0–2 Grid-in = 2–4	• Analysis in History/Social Science ⊙ Reading (Max raw score: 21) ⊙ Writing and Language (Max raw score = 6) ⊙ Math Test (Max raw score = 8) » No Calculator » Calculator • Analysis in Science ⊙ Reading (Max raw score = 21) ⊙ Writing and Language (Max raw score = 6) ⊙ Math Test (Max raw score = 8) » No Calculator » Calculator

Part I:
General Test-Taking
Advice and
Strategies

Chapter 1

What Is Math and Why Do I Need to Study It?

How can it be that mathematics, being after all a product
of human thought which is independent of experience, is
so admirably appropriate to the objects of reality?

—Albert Einstein

Mathematics is the discipline that deals with concepts such as quantity, structure, space, and change. It evolved, through the use of abstraction and logical reasoning, from counting, calculation, measurement, and the study of the shapes and motions of physical objects.

Math takes relevant elements of factual knowledge and, using analytic or critical thinking skills, combines them to solve problems including (believe it or not) those of the following type:

Professor: "Suppose I know three people. The result of multiplying their ages is 36. Your house number equals the sum of their ages. Can you figure out how old each one of them is?"

The student grabs a pencil and starts scribbling numbers on a paper pad. Two minutes later, he goes back to the professor.

Student: "Are you sure you gave me enough information to answer your question?"

The professor, after repeating out loud his own words, replies: "Actually you're right. I forgot to tell you that the oldest one plays the violin."

The student looks back at his worksheet and immediately, with a sigh of relief, gives the professor the correct answer.

(Find the solution in Appendix A on p. 303.)

Why You Should Never Say "I Hate Math!"

Nature is the realization of the simplest conceivable mathematical ideas.

—Albert Einstein

Math is a set of essential life skills that allows us to better understand, make sense, and take advantage of the myriad aspects of the reality in which we live. Real life presents itself as a collection of mundane *problems*, and our ability to solve them plays an essential role in our quest for professional success happiness.

For example, writers, based on their work habits and history, may have to give their publishers an educated guess to help estimate the completion date of their manuscripts. French teachers on field trips to France should use basic arithmetic skills to give students a lecture in home economics with a local flavor, taking into account currency conversion and an understanding of the local tax system. Travel agents might want to be able to estimate the distance between two locations using available maps. Pharmacists, to prepare different dosages of the same medication, would need to understand and apply rules of proportionality to figure out the quantities of various required substances and ingredients that constitute the components of a prescribed drug. Police detectives need good critical thinking skills to put together disparate pieces of the case they are trying to solve and be comfortable with a thinking process that requires multiple iterations and multitasking. Physicists and computer scientists use math concepts as tools that allow them to understand the laws governing physical processes and the machine language and functionality of their computers. And, homemakers can save money by collecting coupons, becoming intelligent buyers, and optimizing their household budgets with good knowledge of and application of concepts such as retail cost, wholesale cost, percentage of discounts, local taxes, shipping and handling charges, and hidden costs.

In its importance, math—being also the science/art of how to put one's knowledge to work in real life—transcends the borders of science and engineering into humanities and all other walks of life. So, even if your goal is to become a history teacher, you will still need math!

Chapter 2

Test Preparation Strategies and Advice

How Too Much "Strategy" Can Be Hazardous to Your Performance

There is only one corner of the universe you can be certain of improving, and that's your own self.

—Aldous Huxley

There is far too much printed advice on "strategy" in approaching test preparation. For the SAT math section, unfortunately, a large percentage of it is based on pseudo/quasiscientific methodologies such as "how to guess right," "how to solve problems via trial and error," and similar tropes. The danger of over emphasizing the importance of strategy is that it shifts attention from the fundamental thing that is required in math preparation—the realization that there is no substitute for the need to acquire the knowledge and skills that are essential in problem solving.

My extensive experience in test preparation has revealed three major areas on which test scores depend: factual knowledge, analytic/critical thinking skills, and concentration skills.

Factual Knowledge

There has not been, is not, and will never be a consensus on how much memorization of factual knowledge is necessary for a well-rounded education. There certainly is a decent body of knowledge that you are expected to master in preparation for the math section of the SAT test. That begins with "simple" concepts (e.g., arithmetic operations, definitions of two-dimensional geometric figures, etc.) and ends with more sophisticated math concepts such as compound probabilities. Average and above-average students are not expected to have significant gaps in their factual knowledge or math background.

Analytic/Critical Thinking Skills

One may refer to these as the glue that keeps together our body of knowledge and the catalyst that gives us the ability to put it to use in solving real-life problems. This is what is missing when a student cannot solve a problem and yet has the same theoretical background as someone who shows him how to solve it. "Gosh, how come I didn't see that?" is the typical reaction, noticing that finding a solution did not require the use of a "magic" formula or, for that matter, any factual knowledge with which the student was not familiar. Possession of these skills is paramount to achieving excellence in any profession, not only in those with mathematical or scientific/engineering orientations. These skills are the main reason why nobody should ever be justified in downplaying the role of math in our general education.

The following problem outlines the importance of analytic skills in problem solving.

Problem 1

Given the triangle shown, select the correct answer from the following:
- (A) Area of triangle is less than 75
- (B) Area of triangle is equal to 75
- (C) Area of triangle is greater than 75
- (D) There is not sufficient data to calculate the area of the triangle.

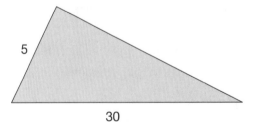

Solution 1

Note that this is basically a quantitative-analysis-type problem that requires that we compare a variable, the area of the triangle, with the number 75.

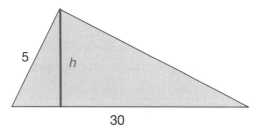

After drawing the height of the triangle (*h*), the formula that gives us the area of the triangle is:

$$\frac{(\text{base} \times \text{height})}{2}$$

The steps described below lead us to a simplification of the problem whereby what we are left to compare is "*h*" and "5" (much better/simpler task than comparing "area of triangle" and "75"). The following comparisons are equivalent:

Area of triangle	vs.	75
$\frac{(30 \times h)}{2}$	vs.	75
$15 \times h$	vs.	75
h	vs.	5

The notations we added to the figure, emphasizing the fact that "*h*" is perpendicular to the base of the triangle, should easily point out the fact that the two elements we need to compare are the sides of the newly created right triangle. Because "*h*" is a side and "5" is the hypotenuse, and because the latter is longer than any of the sides of the triangle, it follows that

$$h < 5$$

and thus the area of the triangle < 75, and the answer is A.

Note that the only factual knowledge required to solve this problem was the formula for the area of a triangle and the property of right triangles, according to which the hypotenuse is the longest of the sides.

Concentration Skills

To understand the role that concentration plays in taking the SAT test, try to answer the question: "When is the last time you sat down and worked on anything for almost 4 hours[2]?" Considering that for most students, a candid answer is "never," one should wonder why there is so little interest in or emphasis on this aspect of test preparation in most preparatory books available on the market.

In my experience, this is the primary reason for underachievement by above-average students (a category that includes the not-doing-well-on-tests type).

If someone wants to run a marathon, that person needs to prepare/practice for it! No matter how good of an athlete a student is in a different sport, running a marathon requires a unique combination of skills in the areas of endurance and effort optimization.

I suggest two ways to address this issue and improve one's concentration skills:

- A time window equal to the duration of the test (3 hours 50 minutes, including the optional essay) should be periodically allotted to taking a complete test. That, of course, would require a distraction-free environment (e.g., no phone calls, background music, snacks, etc.).

- Students should improve or totally change (depending on their working habits) the approach they use in dealing with their homework. Imagine that all homework (say, preparation for a chemistry test, some reading for geography, and a couple of exercises in French) would be treated as one monolithic task. That would require the same distraction-free environment and need to work nonstop until everything that has to do with the next day's homework is accomplished. In this way, not only the quality of homework is expected to increase (with a positive impact on grades), but also the students will be indirectly practicing for their SAT by improving their concentration skills.

A balanced combination of the strategies outlined above has proved to have a positive impact on students' concentration skills.

---

2   The PSAT and SAT tests require 2 hours 45 minutes and 3 hours 50 minutes (the 50–minute essay being optional, respectively.

When Guessing Works

There are always exceptions to the rules!

Even for educators who do not give much credit to a correct answer without first seeing the student's work, the reality of the test's time constraints and its current structure/format simply make it impossible not to mention guessing as a needed strategy.

As a result, and again given that penalties for wrong answers no longer apply, it is *strongly recommended that multiple-choice problems not be omitted*. After all, any guess would give the student a 25% chance (1 in 4) of picking the right answer. Time permitting, students should make an effort to rule out as many answers/options as possible, narrowing down the odds to 1 in 3 or 1 in 2, and thus increasing their chances of picking the correct answer from 25% to 33.3% or even 50%.

An Approach to Test Preparation

Those are my principles, and if you don't like them . . . well, I have others.

—Groucho Marx

The "Test-After-Test" Approach

This is the most common approach to test preparation, and it involves either taking "mock" tests or solving problems from disparate sections of real tests using books such those published by the College Entrance Examination Board. The former allows you to emulate the test experience by taking complete tests within the actual test's time limit.

In addition to the problem-solving experience and the exposure to the wide range of math topics and degrees of difficulty, this approach also is useful for allowing you to get a glimpse into the "real thing" and experience the impact of time constraints on your performance.

The "Identification of Weaknesses/Gaps" Approach

Books like those published by Barron's offer students a set of tools that while complementing the "test-after-test" approach also should fill in the gaps and add more efficiency to the test preparation process.

Books that use this approach take the math required for the test and group it by topics. Major topics are then divided up into subtopics, each of which is prefaced by a summary of the theoretical concepts involved. This way, you do not have to rely on different textbooks for refreshing your memory. Following that, exercises and problems dealing with that particular topic are given to complete the preparation-by-topic exercise. Books that group by topic (this one included) distinguishes itself by offering a good selection of real problems (i.e., problems given in real tests), grouped by topic and type (i.e., multiple choice and open-ended), and by—occasionally—adding a challenge component by dropping most of the problems that in a real test would be considered "easy." This should be seen as good news because it gives students the opportunity to challenge themselves in the preparatory environment, making the real test an easier than expected examination experience.

This "targeted" approach should be used to identify weaknesses and gaps in theory, problem content, and problem types. It is extremely useful in adding efficiency to the process of test preparation, especially if you have already taken the test once and you're concentrating on improving your scores. In the time spent for preparation between test dates, emphasis should be on how to maximize the efficiency of the time spent to improve performance.

Last but not least, the partnership between Khan Academy and College Board provides students with free online help on various math topics and techniques.

The "Take-the-Challenge" Approach

You should constantly challenge yourself when preparing for the SAT. Here are some suggestions:

- Skip problems that look easy and/or revolve around topics with which you are comfortable.
- When practicing working on a section of a real test, skip the "easy" problems.
- Solve more word and open-ended problems (i.e., problems that traditionally fall into the hard category).
- Solve more problems on topics that are not easy; statistically, these could be topics such as probabilities, geometric and arithmetic sequences, Venn diagrams, and so forth.

I recommend all of the above techniques be used alternatively. However, the time ratio spent on using them should be slightly in favor of a combination of the second and third approaches with a more accurate ratio depending on your specific needs that you or your instructor/tutor have detected.

Do Calculators Really Help?

Man's mind stretched by a new idea never goes back to its original dimensions.
—Oliver Wendell Holmes

None of the math problems given on the old SAT were designed to require the use of a calculator, yet calculators were allowed. The math in the new SAT is clearly divided into two sections: a "no-calculator" one (Section 3) and one that allows the use of calculators (Section 4.) This can be seen as an effort to minimize students' reliance on calculators.

Given the degree of difficulty of SAT problems (past and present) and the typical calculations required in obtaining the correct solutions, it is doubtful that calculators would help students solve the problems more quickly. In addition, they can be seen as a hindrance to the thinking process and a potential long-term hazard because of their "addictive" nature.

The popular belief is that calculators help us solve problems in less time than what we would need without using them. In the case of SAT problems, this is not true for the most part.

A student taking the SAT test is like a marathon runner. He or she will be engaged in an endurance exercise and success depends very much on her ability to perform consistently well for the whole duration of the test. Setting aside the mental preparation involved, marathon runners need to warm up their muscles and bring them to a level of performance that can be sustained for the entire duration of the race. When they feel dehydrated, for example, they do not stop to take a sip of water but rather grab a cup held out to them by officials and drink it while continuing to run at the same pace. Stopping would be extremely detrimental to them, as it would cool off the muscles and change the body chemistry to the one required when resting, and getting back into the race would require starting the whole cycle from the beginning, making them lose precious time and stamina.

Being engaged in a mental/intellectual exercise, such as taking an SAT test, is, in many ways, analogous to running a marathon. When it comes to "warming up" and sustaining the effort for the duration of the exercise, it is our "neurons," our mind, that need to carry us throughout the 3-hour-plus test maintaining the same (a constant) high level of concentration and performance ability. Each time we make use of a calculator, we stop the thinking process.

As an example, consider the following problem:

Problem 2

$$\frac{1}{2} \times \frac{2}{3} \times \frac{3}{4} \times \frac{4}{5} \times \frac{5}{6} \times \frac{6}{7} =$$

Solution 2

The students who tend to make too much use of calculators would waste no time and start calculating the above expression without paying any attention to the numerators and denominators of the above fractions. That is an example where too much reliance on calculators becomes a hindrance to the thinking process. A quick glimpse at the fractions in question should result in the observation that all but one denominator and numerator remain (i.e., "7" and "1," respectively) after the others were cancelled off diagonally.

$$\frac{1}{\cancel{2}} \times \frac{\cancel{2}}{\cancel{3}} \times \frac{\cancel{3}}{\cancel{4}} \times \frac{\cancel{4}}{\cancel{5}} \times \frac{\cancel{5}}{\cancel{6}} \times \frac{\cancel{6}}{7} = \frac{1}{7}$$

In addition, using the calculator for simple operations that we could do in our heads (a) makes us hesitant and increases our dependency on calculators and (b) gives our mind, presumably warmed up for the mental exercise of taking the test, an unnecessary and detrimental break. Problem 9 (see p. 30) is another example that can be used to back up the argument against exaggerated use of calculators.

This being said, students will occasionally find in the *calculator section* of the new SAT problems that would require simple multiplications of divisions of numbers (integers or even decimals) where the use of a calculator could be justified, as it would save a few seconds in calculating the correct solution. Was the calculator really needed? I'll leave it up to the reader to decide. Problem 3 is an example of this.

Problem 3

A take-out restaurant sells subs for $4.50 each and drinks for $1.50. An order of subs and drinks for a company barbeque totaled $345. That represented the cost of 130 subs and drinks. How many subs were ordered for the party?

Solution 3

If the number of subs and drinks purchased for the party are denoted with S and D, respectively, the following set of two equations summarizes the data given above:

$$4.5S + 1.5D = 345$$
$$S + D = 130$$

Using the *elimination technique*, we multiply the second equation by –1.5 and rewrite it as
$$-1.5S - 1.5D = 130 \times (-1.5) = -195$$

By adding this equation to the first unchanged equation, the term in D cancels out and we have
$$3S = 345 - 195 = 150 \quad \text{or} \quad S = \frac{150}{3} = 50.$$

Too Much Memorization?

Intelligence is not the ability to store information, but to know where to find it.

—Albert Einstein

There is a popular belief that memory is extremely important in solving math problems. Many times, this complements the idea (popular with those who do not quite see a connection between algebra and the real world) that algebra is an abstract, stand-alone science.

Both theories must be taken with a grain of salt. Although some memorization is needed in order to acquire the required body of math knowledge, a thorough understanding of the fundamentals should lead to a more lasting mastery of math concepts. Understanding the definitions, and how certain concepts, rules, and theorems were derived and the rationale behind them, should eliminate the excessive reliance on memory.

As an example, let us consider the task of calculating the sum of interior angles of any two-dimensional, geometric figure (i.e., a polygon). The only thing that we need to remember is what the answer would be should the polygon have three sides (i.e., be a triangle): 180°. Then, the area of the polygon should be divided up into triangles. It does not matter where and how we start. The sum of the interior angles of the polygon is equal to the number of triangles obtained times 180°. This shows that memorizing the formula, $(n - 1) \times 180°$, where n = number of sides, is not necessary, as we can derive it easily using the approach described above (also see Problem 58).

I strongly recommend that you make an effort to apply logic in understanding various math concepts and rely less on rote memorization, which may lead to a mechanical approach to problem solving.

Ubiquitous Algebra

Q: So how do you find America? A: Turn left at Greenland.

—John Lennon

As a testimony to the importance of algebra is the fact that about 1/3 of all SAT problems fall under the "heart of algebra" category.

Algebra, far from being an abstract, stand-alone science, should be seen as a set of tools that mathematicians have devised to help them (and us) solve real-life problems. These are the problems (and a vast majority of problems fall into this category) that invariably require a translation of the text into a language better suited to capture and summarize all information given to us in a succinct form (i.e., allow translation of English to algebra).

This paradigm, while emphasizing the importance of algebraic skills, leads to a three-step approach to problem solving:

1. Read the problem, define the unknowns/variables, and identify them with letters (e.g., x, y, z).
2. With the notations introduced at Step #1, translate the text of the problem into algebra by writing the relationships between known and unknown data (i.e., the equations).
3. Solve the equations using techniques learned in algebra (e.g., substitution or elimination).

See Problem 4 for an example.

Problem 4

Anna has 5 times as many marbles as Bob. If Anna gives Bob 7 marbles, Anna will be left with 6 more marbles than Bob. What is the total number of marbles that Anna and Bob have?

Solution 4

1. Let the number of marbles originally in Anna's and Bob's possession be A and B, respectively.
2. Translation of the first sentence leads to:

$$A = 5 \times B$$

Translation of the second sentence leads to:

$$A - 7 = B + 7 + 6$$

3. We are now left with the easier task (after simplifying and rearranging the second equation in Step #2) of solving the following set of equations:

$$A = 5 \times B$$
$$A = B + 20$$

Solving by substitution leads to $5B = B + 20$, or $4B = 20$, or

$$B = 5 \text{ and } A = 25$$

The result $(A + B)$ is 30.

On Your Own Problem 1*

A bag contains black, white, and red marbles. The number of white marbles is 2 more than the number of black marbles, and the number of red marbles is 4 times the number of white marbles. Which of the following could be the total number of marbles in the bag?

(A) 53
(B) 48
(C) 26
(D) 46

---

*   Check your answer against the correct one shown in Appendix B (p. 305).

Fast Math

Sometimes it's a little better to travel than to arrive.

—Robert Pirsig

Many students have a "timing" problem. Some can solve most of the SAT problems but tend to never be able to finish the math sections in the time allotted by the College Board (25 and 55 minutes for Section 3 and 4, respectively). Keep in mind that, on average, a student will only have a little less than a minute and a half per problem (see also Table 9, p. 37). As such, speeding up problem solving becomes essential and to achieve it, I suggest a two-prong strategy.

Common Approach

A common approach to problem solving saves time by minimizing the transition time intervals between problems dealing with different topics. Whether the problem is about solving a set of equations (algebra) or involves angle relationships in a geometric figure (geometry) or probabilities, if we could approach it in the same way (i.e., via a process involving the same sequence of logical steps), we will be saving time!

One way to standardize the way we solve math problems is by dividing up the work into three distinct tasks:

- read and understand well the information/data provided;
- identify variables that together with the information/data provided are relevant to and will play a role in solving the problem; and
- define a strategy/approach to problem solving based on input data and relevant variables, then implement it.

The first task is a crucial step in solving math problems and, most of the time, when one is not able to do so (i.e., one gets stuck in the middle of the problem), the reason is that some relevant information was left out or misunderstood.

Note that the ability to accomplish the third task either in its entirety or in a timely manner has a lot to do with how well the input data was understood, captured, and summarized either in memory or, preferably, on paper. An example of such a strategy is shown in the previous section, where the concept of translation of English to algebra is discussed and illustrated in Problem 44.

See the next few problems for more examples:

Problem 5

A soccer team has played 20 games and has won 40% of them. What is the minimum number of additional games the team must win to finish the season winning 75% of the games it has played?

Solution 5

Relevant Data/Information:

- number of games played = 20
- percentage of wins = 40%
- goal: percentage of wins = 75%
- need to calculate *minimum* number of additional games

Variables:

- let *w* be the number of initial wins (that led to the 40% performance)
- let *n* be the number of additional games to be played that, consistent with the meaning given by using the adjective *minimum* above, also are "wins"

With this information, we can begin to solve the problem:

$$40\% = \frac{40}{100} = \frac{4}{10} = \frac{2}{5} = \frac{\#\,wins\,(initial)}{\#\,games\,(initial)} = \frac{w}{20}$$

$$w = \frac{20 \times 2}{5} = 8$$

$$75\% = \frac{75}{100} = \frac{3}{4} = \frac{\#\,wins\,(initial+final)}{\#\,games\,(initial+final)} = \frac{8+n}{20+n}$$

$$60 + 3n = 32 + 4n$$

$$60 - 32 = n$$

$$n = 28$$

Thus, to improve its wining performance from 40% to 75%, the team will have to play (and win) 28 additional games.

Problem 6

In the geometric figure shown below, $\overline{AC}$ is perpendicular to $\overline{BD}$, $AC = 20$ and $BD = 25$. Calculate the area of $ABCD$.

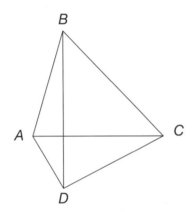

Solution 6

Relevant Data/Information:
- AC is perpendicular to BD
- $AC = 20$
- $BD = 25$

Variables:

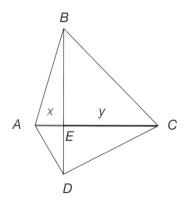

- $x = AE$
- $y = EC$

The area of $ABCD$ can be calculated as the sum of the areas of two triangles, either (1) $\triangle ABD$ and $\triangle DBC$ or (2) $\triangle ABC$ and $\triangle ACD$. This is a symmetrical problem and as such, either approach will lead to the correct answer.

Assume we pursue option (1): area of $ABCD$ = area of $\triangle ABD$ + area of $\triangle DBC$, or

$$A_{ABCD} = A_{\triangle ABD} + A_{\triangle BDC} = \frac{BD \times x}{2} = \frac{BD \times y}{2} = \frac{BD \times (x+y)}{2} = \frac{25 \times 20}{2} = 250$$

where x and y are the heights of triangles ABD and DBC respectively, and $x + y = AC = 20$

Problem 7

Eric's average of four tests is 90. Which of the following cannot be the number of tests on which he earned exactly 90 points?

(A) 0
(B) 1
(C) 2
(D) 3

Solution 7

Relevant Data/Information:
- the average of 4 tests is 90
- the answer must represent the number of tests whose score *cannot be exactly* 90

Variables:
- let the 4 test scores be $t1, t2, t3, t4$

Let's apply the definition of average:

$$\frac{t1 + t2 + t3 + t4}{4} = 90$$

or

$$t1 + t2 + t3 + t4 = 4 \times 90 = 360$$

By elimination (starting with A), we rule out "0," "1," and "2" as—in each case—we can easily find 4, 3, and 2 numbers, respectively, whose sum is 360 and that are different from 90.

If "D" were the answer, then

$$t1 = t2 = t3 = 90$$

and

$$t1 + t2 + t3 = 3 \times 90 = 270$$

or

$$t4 = 360 - 270 = 90$$

Thus, the fourth score would also be 90, validating D (3) as the unique solution.

Minimum Calculations

Most problems rated "medium" or "hard" cannot be solved in one step. In the new SAT the number and importance of multistep problems has also increased. In those cases, calculations, when possible, should not be done at every intermediate step but rather carried over to the very last logical step of the solution. When pursuing this strategy, the total number of calculations per problem will be dramatically reduced (primarily as a result of reductions/cancellations). As a consequence, the odds of making a mistake will diminish (fewer calculations/operations = fewer mistakes) and the overall timing will be reduced.

Problem 8

If 700 pounds of hay will feed 30 cows for 2 weeks, for how many days will 300 pounds of hay feed 6 cows?

    (A) 10
    (B) 20
    (C) 30
    (D) 40

Solution 8

Observation #1: For constant number of days during which food supplies are sufficient, the quantity of food and number of days are directly proportional quantities ("more food, more days").

Observation #2: If quantity of food is constant, the number of cows and number of days are inversely proportional quantities ("more cows, fewer days").

We'll set up the problem in a manner that outlines the relationship (direct proportionality) among quantity of hay, number of cows, and number of days:

700 [lb] $\longrightarrow$ 30 [# cows] $\longrightarrow$ 14 [days]

Because these quantities are directly/inversely proportional, one can write

1 [lb] $\longrightarrow$ 30 [# cows] $\longrightarrow$ $\dfrac{14}{700}$ [days]

1 [lb] $\longrightarrow$ 1 [# cows] $\longrightarrow$ $\dfrac{14 \times 30}{700}$ [days]

$$1 \text{ [lb]} \longrightarrow 6 \text{ [\# cows]} \longrightarrow \frac{14 \times 30}{700 \times 6} \text{ [days]}$$

$$300 \text{ [lb]} \longrightarrow 6 \text{ [\# cows]} \longrightarrow \frac{14 \times 30 \times 300}{700 \times 6} \text{ [days]}$$

Note that all calculations have been postponed until the last step. It is now easy to see how simplifications can reduce calculations to a minimum, in this case to "no" calculations at all as simplifying the fraction should not require a calculator:

$$\frac{14 \times 30 \times 300}{700 \times 6} = 2 \times 5 \times 3 = 30$$

Thus, the correct answer is C.

Problem 9

If each factor in the product shown below has the form

$$\left(1 + \frac{1}{k}\right),$$

where k represents all of the consecutive integers from 2 to 19, what is the value of P?

$$P = \left(1 + \frac{1}{2}\right)\left(1 + \frac{1}{3}\right)\left(1 + \frac{1}{4}\right)\cdots\left(1 + \frac{1}{19}\right)$$

Solution 9

Rewrite a few factors at the beginning and at the end of the expression given for *P*:

$$P = \frac{3}{2} \times \frac{4}{3} \times \frac{5}{4} \times \ldots \times \frac{18}{17} \times \frac{19}{18} \times \frac{20}{19} = \frac{20}{2} = 10$$

By simplifying/reducing the fractions—as shown above—with no need to use a calculator, the number of calculations is reduced to one: 20/2. The answer, therefore, is 10.

Reading Comprehension

There is an overlap between the skills required to solve certain math problems (e.g., word problems) and the reading comprehension skills emphasized in various aspects of the verbal ("Evidence-Based Reading and Writing") sections of the SAT test. As a result, poor reading comprehension skills will have a negative impact on the math score, in particular in the students' ability to solve "hard," open-ended, and word problems.

PSAT Versus SAT

Confusion of goals and perfection of means seems,
in my opinion, to characterize our age.

—Albert Einstein

The Preliminary SAT (PSAT) implies that this test is meant to give the student a preliminary idea of how well he or she will do on the SAT[3]. Although the PSAT is indeed designed as a warm-up for the SAT, it has taken on an importance of its own because of its use by the National Merit Program. Hence, one sees the acronym NMSQT (National Merit Scholarship Qualifying Test) alongside PSAT[4].

The following is an attempt to succinctly characterize the difference between the PSAT and SAT.

---

3   In this book, SAT is used to designate the "SAT I" test as opposed to "SAT II" (i.e., the "general" as opposed to the "subject" test).
4   As in PSAT/NMSQT.

General

The PSAT is a preparatory/practice tool for the SAT. Its capability to assess students' skills at a given point in time and, in particular, its capacity to predict their performance on the SAT, while widely advertised, are controversial claims still open for debate.

The NMSQT factor is probably the most important reason for students to consider taking the PSAT. High scorers on the PSAT (≥ 95th percentile) may qualify for a National Merit Scholarship and Letters of Commendations, prestigious achievements that would certainly enhance a college applicant's chances for admission.

Prepare for the PSAT

The math contents of PSAT and SAT are—for the most part—similar. The PSAT is known to exclude some topics that a majority of first-semester juniors have not covered, most notably (some) Algebra II-type problems.

Given that the PSAT (1) requires much of the same factual knowledge[5] and (2) has the same question types (multiple-choice and grid-in/open-ended), virtually all of the preparatory strategies and techniques that apply to the SAT also apply to the PSAT. (That explains the absence of books dedicated exclusively to PSAT preparation!)

The average SAT problem has a slightly higher level of difficulty than its PSAT counterpart and is therefore more challenging. Like in sports, accept the challenge and the results will award you for that (not to mention getting an early start on preparation for the "ultimate" test: the SAT).

Content, Timing, and Scoring

Content wise, these two tests pretty much mirror each other, with the SAT rightfully claiming a slightly higher level of difficulty. To quantify it in detail and in an objective way is, surprisingly, not a trivial matter. What does not seem to be a matter of interpretation, though, is the characterization that "the SAT is a more difficult test than the PSAT" because:

- The optional essay on the SAT is not an option on the PSAT.
- Although difficult Algebra II problems are few on the SAT, they are absent altogether on the PSAT.
- The SAT is longer than the PSAT (see Table 7) and thus requires better concentration skills and stamina.
- The structure of the "new" PSAT mirrors the one used for the "new" SAT. Table 7 provides some specifics in the areas of timing and content.

---

5   The College Board—to this author's knowledge—has never made available a list of math topics that are covered in the SAT but not in the PSAT or, for that matter, quantifiable information on the difference in the order of difficulty between PSAT and SAT math problems.

TABLE 7

PSAT Versus SAT

			PSAT Versus SAT			
			Time		Number of Questions	
			PSAT	SAT	PSAT	SAT
Evidence-Based Reading and Writing	Reading		60	65	47	52
	Writing and Language		35	35	44	44
Math	No Calculator	mc	25	25	13	15
		oe			4	5
	Calculator	mc	45	55	27	30
		oe			4	8
Total			2h45min	3h	139	154

The scorings of the two tests—in the new format—were lined up to make it easier for students taking the PSAT to use its score as a predictor of their performance in the SAT. As a result, the same scoring model is used: total score (split equally between Evidence-Based Reading and Writing and Math), subscores (4 and 3 in Evidence-Based Reading and Writing and Math, respectively), and cross-test scores (2 in Analysis in History/Social Studies and Analysis in Science).

The score ranges in math are 160–760 and 200–800 in PSAT and SAT (with total score ranges of 320–1520 and 400–1600), respectively.

SAT Versus ACT

Although the changes implemented by the College Board in 2016 reduced the gap between the SAT and the ACT, differences remain. In contrast to the format of the SAT (shown in Tables 1 and 2), the content of the ACT is described below:

ACT ("American College Test"): General Information

Section 1: English test.
Description: Measures student's understanding of the conventions of standard written English (e.g., punctuation, sentence structure, grammar, and usage)

Number of questions: 75 (5 passages x 15 questions/passage)

Time: 45 minutes

Format: Passage-based; multiple-choice questions with four choices per question

Score(s):

Total (1–36)
Subscore 1 (1–18): Usage/mechanics
Subscore 2 (1–18): Rhetorical skills

Miscellaneous: Does not really test spelling, vocabulary, and grammar rules

Section 2: Math test.

Description: Measures student's understanding of pre-, elementary, and intermediate algebra, coordinate and plane geometry, and trigonometry requiring knowledge of basic formulas and computational skills

Number of questions: 60

Time: 60 minutes

Format: Multiple-choices questions with five choices per question

Score(s):

Total (1–36)
Subscore 1 (1–18): Prealgebra and elementary algebra
Subscore 2 (1–18): Intermediate algebra and coordinate geometry
Subscore 3 (1–18): Plane geometry and trigonometry

Miscellaneous: Use of "approved" calculators is permitted, however, none of the math problems should really require the use of a calculator; recollection of complex formulas and/or extensive computation is not required

Section 3: Reading test.

Description: Measures student's reading comprehension skills

Number of questions: 40 (4 passages x 10 questions/passage)

Time: 35 minutes

Format: Passage-based; multiple-choice with four choices per question

Score(s):

Total (1–36)
Subscore 1 (1–18): Social studies/natural sciences (20 questions)
Subscore 2 (1–18): Arts and literature (20 questions)

Miscellaneous: Students are expected to derive meaning from the given passages by referring to what is explicitly stated and by reasoning (i.e., determining the implicit meaning)

Section 4: Science test.

Description: Measures student's interpretation/evaluation, analytic/reasoning, and problem-solving skills required in natural sciences (biology, chemistry, Earth/space sciences, and physics)

Number of questions: 40 (7 passages x 5/6/7 questions/passage)

Time: 35 minutes

Format: Passage-based; multiple-choice with four choices per question

Score(s):

Total (1–36)

Miscellaneous: Understanding scientific terms/concepts is required; advanced knowledge in the various topics of natural sciences is not required; content: data representation (30%–40%), research summaries (45%–55%), conflicting viewpoints (15%–20%)

Optional: Writing test.

Description: A measure of student's writing skills and ability to develop his or her own perspective with regard to a given topic

Time: 40 minutes

Format: Essay

Score(s):

Total (1–36)
Subscore 1 (1–36): English language
Subscore 2 (2–12): Ideas and analysis
Subscore 3 (2–12): Development and support
Subscore 4 (2–12): Organization
Subscore 5 (2–12): Language use and conventions

Miscellaneous: Students are expected to establish and explain the relationship between their perspective (on the topic) and the ones given

With regard to math, Tables 3 and 4 (SAT data) should be compared to Table 8.

A further comparison between the two tests is illustrated in Table 9.

Given the difference between the scoring methodologies used in SAT and ACT, colleges (a majority of whom accept both tests) would have to rely on concordance tables such as the one in Table 10 (published by the College Board on May 9, 2016).

TABLE 8

ACT Math Content

Subscore Areas	Topic (% of Test/ No. of Questions)	Content
Prealgebra and Elementary Algebra	Prealgebra (23%/14)	• Operations using whole numbers, integers, decimals, fractions • Integer powers and square roots • Ratio, proportion, percent • Multiples and factors of integers • Absolute value • Number line (ordering numbers) • Linear equations with one variable • Counting principle and simple probabilities • Data representation and interpretation (in charts, tables, graphs) • Basic statistics (mean, median, mode)
	Elementary Algebra (17%/10)	• Expressing relationships using variables • Substituting variables in expressions • Basic operations with and factoring polynomials • Solving quadratic equations (by factoring) • Solving linear inequalities with one variable • Properties of integer exponents and square roots
Intermediate Algebra and Coordinate Geometry	Intermediate Algebra (15%/9)	• Quadratic formula • Radical and rational expressions • Inequalities and absolute value equations • Sequences • Systems of equations • Quadratic inequalities • Functions • Matrices • Roots of polynomials • Complex numbers
	Coordinate Geometry (15%/9)	• Real number line • Standard (x,y) coordinate plane • Representation of points, lines, polynomials, circles, and other curves in the (x,y) coordinate plane • Relationships between equations and graphs • Slope • Parallel and perpendicular lines • Distance (formula) and midpoints • Transformations • Conics
Plane Geometry and Trigonometry	Plane Geometry (23%/14)	• Properties and relations of plane figures (triangles, rectangles, parallelograms, trapezoids, circles) • Angles, parallel and perpendicular lines • Translations, rotations, reflections • Proof techniques • Simple three-dimensional geometry • Perimeter, area, volume • Justification, proof, logical conclusions
	Trigonometry (7%/4)	• Trigonometric ratios (for right triangles) • Values, properties, graphs of trigonometric functions • Trigonometric identities • Trigonometric equations • Modeling with trigonometric functions

TABLE 9

SAT Versus ACT

	SAT[1]	ACT
Structure	Section 1: Reading Test Section 2: Writing and Language Test Section 3: Math Test—No Calculator Section 4: Math Test—Calculator Optional Essay	Section 1: English Test Section 2: Math Test Section 3: Reading Test Section 4: Science Test Optional Essay
Total Testing Time	3 hours + 50-minute essay	2 hours 55 minutes + 40-minute essay
Total Number of Questions	154	215
Time Per Questions	70 seconds	49 seconds
Tests Length and Timing	Reading Test: 52 questions/65 minutes Writing and Language Test: 44 questions/35 minutes Math Test—No Calculator: 20 questions/25 minutes Math Test—Calculator: 38 questions/55 minutes	English Test: 75 questions/45 minutes Math Test: 60 questions/60 minutes Reading Test: 40 questions/35 minutes Science Test: 40 questions/35 minutes
Scoring	Composite: 400–1600 Subscores: 2 Area Scores (200–800)[2] 3 Test Scores (10–40)[3] 2 Cross-Test Scores (10–40)[4] 7 Subscores (1–15)[5]	Composite: 1–36 Subscores: 2 English (1–18)[6] 3 Math (1–18)[7] 2 reading (1–18)[8]
Types of Questions	Multiple choice (4 choices) and Open-ended	Multiple choice (5 choices)

1　Refers to the test format adopted since March 2016
2　Evidence-Based Reading and Writing + Math
3　Reading + Writing and Language + Math
4　Analysis in Science + History/Social Studies
5　Command of Evidence + Relevant Words in Context + Expression of Ideas + Standard English Conventions + Heart of Algebra + Problem Solving and Data Analysis + Passport to Advance Math
6　Usage/Mechanics + Rhetorical Skills
7　Prealgebra and Elementary Algebra + Intermediate Algebra and Coordinate Geometry + Plane Geometry and Trigonometry
8　Social Studies/Natural Sciences (20 questions) + Arts & Literature (20 questions)

TABLE 10

"New" SAT Total to ACT Composite Score Concordance Table
(College Board, 2016)

SAT	1600	1570	1540	1500	1470	1430	1400	1360	1320	1290	1260	1220	1180
ACT	36	35	34	33	32	31	30	29	28	27	26	25	24
SAT	1140	1110	1070	1030	990	950	910	870	830	780	740	680	590
ACT	23	22	21	20	19	18	17	16	15	14	13	12	11

Although the topics (factual knowledge) covered by the two tests are essentially the same (and were earlier summarized in Table 9), here's a summary of the most important differences in math:

- The math sections of the SAT and the ACT account for 1/2 and 1/4 of the total score, respectively.
- The SAT features multiple-choice as well as open-ended problems, whereas the ACT contains only multiple-choice questions.
- The multiple-choice questions in the SAT and the ACT give students four and five choices/options, respectively.
- There are fewer geometry problems in the SAT than in the ACT.
- The SAT gives students more time to answer a question than the ACT (approximately 1.4 second versus 1 second, respectively).
- The SAT has more problems that require data analysis than the ACT (but eventually, the ACT has questions that require data analysis in its Science Test).
- Students are not allowed to use a calculator in one of the two math sections of the SAT whereas use of a calculator is permitted for all ACT math questions.

Final Tips for Better Learning

- Use pencil and scratch paper.
- Constantly identify your weaknesses and gaps; you really want to allocate more time dealing with them.
- What you do at school (or in any afterschool test preparatory environment) should complement work done at home (i.e., it's not a substitute for it!).
- Be candid with yourself (it is so easy to be in denial!) and, if applicable, your instructor/tutor; there is no such thing as a "stupid question"!
- Challenge yourself constantly; make it "harder" during the preparation stages so that the real test will appear "easier" than anticipated; be creative in trying to do so by spending more time solving "hard" problems (e.g., open-ended problems tend to be in that category and so are word problems).
- If you are confident in your mastery of theory, skip it! Solve Problems 10 through 89 in Part II of this book and read the theory (and/or go over examples) *only* when you have second thoughts on how good your understanding of that particular topic is.
- When you cannot work out the correct answer, narrow down the field of choices that make sense and take your pick among them, but try not

to skip any question (even a wild guess on a multiple-choice problem gives you a 25% chance to have picked the correct answer).

- Last but not least: Read books! You'll increase your reading comprehension skills.

Part II: Specific Math Topics, Tips for Problem Solving, and Sample Problems

Chapter 3

Arithmetic Concepts

You cannot teach a man anything; you can only help him discover it in himself.

—Galileo Galilei

3.1: Integer[10]

Definition: Integers are whole numbers, their negatives, and zero.
Example: . . . , -3, -2, -1, 0, 1, 2, 3, . . .

Integers are useful in comparing a direction associated with certain events. Suppose I take five steps forward: This could be viewed as a positive 5. If instead, I take 8 steps backward, we might consider this a -8. Temperature is another way negative numbers are used. On a cold day, the temperature might be 10 degrees Celsius below zero, or -10°C.

We can compare two different integers by looking at their positions on the number line (see Section 3.4). For any two different places on the number line, the integer on the right is greater than the integer on the left. Note that every positive integer is greater than any negative integer. For example:

$$6 > -9 \quad -2 > -8 \quad 0 > -5 \quad -2 < 1 \quad 8 < 11 \quad -7 < -5 \quad -10 < 0$$

---

10   This book uses a number system to delineate the various math topics we'll be covering. When you take the practice test and create an analysis of your results, you'll receive recommendations that will show you which numbered sections of the book you can revisit to try to improve your score.

3.2: Odd/Even Numbers

Definition: An odd number is an integer that is not divisible by 2. An even number is an integer divisible by 2 (without a remainder). Note that even numbers *include* 0.

Examples:

Odd: ..., -5, -3, -1, 1, 3, 5, ...

Even: ..., -4, -2, 0, 2, 4, ...

Here are a few hints to remember about odd and even numbers:
- odd × odd = odd
- even × even = even
- odd × even = even × odd = even

3.3: Consecutive Integers

Definition: Integers that follow in sequence, where the difference between two successive integers is 1.

Example: . . . -3, -2, -1, 0, 1, 2, 3, . . .

Representation of
consecutive integers $x, x + 1, x + 2, x + 3, ...$
consecutive even/odd integers $x, x + 2, x + 4, x + 6, ...$

Problem 10

Given three consecutive integers, if the sum of the first and third integers is increased by 8, the result is 5 less than triple the second integer. Find the three consecutive integers.

$$(x)(x+1)(x+2)$$
$$(x+2)+(x)+8 = (x+1)3-5$$
$$2x+10 = 3x-2$$
$$12 = x$$

$$12, 13, 14$$

Solution 10

Let the three consecutive integers be x, $x + 1$, $x + 2$. Translating the first sentence to algebra leads to:

$$x + (x + 2) + 8 = 3(x + 1) - 5$$
$$2x + 10 = 3x - 2$$
$$\text{or}$$
$x = 12$, with the three consecutive integers being 12, 13, and 14

3.4: Number Line

Definition: A line used to graphically represent the relationships between numbers: integers, fractions, or decimals. On this line, a number is placed in relation to other numbers.

Example:

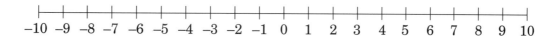

Note that numbers always increase as one moves to the right.

Problem 11

If $p + 1$ is a multiple of 3, what is the greatest multiple of 3 that is less than $p + 1$?

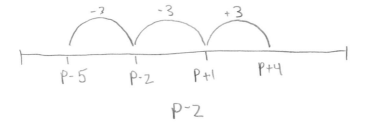

Solution 11

This is one of those "easy" problems that good students have difficulty solving as, many times, great minds have a tendency to complicate things more than one should (i.e., to overanalyze).

The keys to solving this problem are:

- coming to grips with the fact that "$p + 1$" is a number and students should not try to solve for "p," and
- understanding the importance (in the context of this problem) of the adjective "greatest."

Placing the number ($p + 1$) on a number line (see diagram below) is strongly encouraged, as it will provide instant help, especially to those who have a good visual memory.

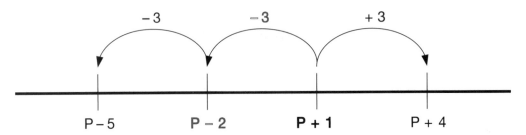

By illustrating the position of a few consecutive multiples of 3 (to include $p + 1$) and the mechanics of shifting from a particular one to the preceding or the next one, it is easy to pick the correct answer: The "greatest multiple of 3 that is less than $p + 1$" is $p - 2$.

Problem 12

If $n + 1$ is a multiple of 5, what is the smallest multiple of 5 that is greater than $n + 1$?

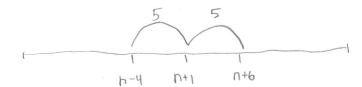

Solution 12

The previous multiple of 5 on the number line, or the "greatest multiple of 5 that is less than $n + 1$" is

$$n + 1 - 5 = n - 4$$

The next multiple of 5 on the number line—the "smallest multiple of 5 that is greater than $n + 1$"—is obtained by adding 5:

$$n + 1 + 5 = n + 6$$

On Your Own Problem 2

The coordinates of two points on the number line are shown below. Calculate the value of x if the distance between the points is 4.

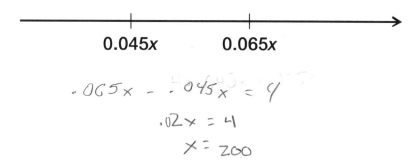

0.045x   0.065x

$.065x - .045x = 4$

$.02x = 4$

$x = 200$

On Your Own Problem 3

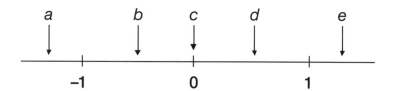

The location of numbers a, b, c, d, and e on the number line is shown above. Out of the quantities (products) shown below, indicate which one has the least value.

(A) a

(B) ab

(C) ac

(D) ae

3.5: Reciprocal (of a Number)

Definition: One number is reciprocal of another number if their product is 1 (i.e., the reciprocal of a number = 1 divided by the number).

Example: Reciprocal of x is $\frac{1}{x}$

Problem 13

Find the reciprocal of $\frac{3}{7}$.

$$\frac{1}{3/7} = \frac{7}{3} = 2\,\tfrac{1}{3}$$

Solution 13

$$\frac{1}{\frac{3}{7}} = \frac{7}{3} = 2\frac{1}{3}$$

3.6: Factors (of a Number)

Definition: Positive integers that can evenly be divided into the number (i.e., there is no remainder).

Example: The factors of 36 are: 1, 2, 3, 4, 6, 9, 12, 18, 36 (i.e., the numbers that can be divided evenly into 36 or the numbers that 36 is divisible by).

Problem 14

What are the factors of 84?

$$84 < \begin{matrix} 2 \\ 42 \end{matrix} < \begin{matrix} 2 \\ 21 \end{matrix} < \begin{matrix} 7 \\ 3 \end{matrix}$$

Solution 14

The factors of 84 are: 1 (a factor of everything); 2, 3, 7 (the distinct prime factors; we actually have 2 twice; see below and also the section on prime numbers); 4, 6, 14, 21 (products of two prime factors); 12, 28, 42 (products of three prime factors); and 84 (product of all the prime factors). A diagram can help to explain this, as shown below.

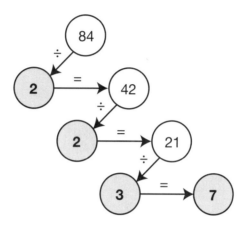

3.7: Common Factors

Definition: Factors that two (or more) numbers have in common.
Examples:
The factors of 12 are: 1, 2, 3, 4, 6, 12
The factors of 36 are: 1, 2, 3, 4, 6, 12, 18, 36
Common factors of 12 and 36 are: 1, 2, 3, 4, 6, 12

See next topic for sample problems.

3.8: Greatest Common Factor (GCF)

Definition: The largest common factor of two (or more) numbers.
Example: GCF of 12 and 36 is 12

Problem 15

Find the GCF of 36 and 54.

$36 < \begin{matrix} 12 < \begin{matrix} 3 \\ 4 < \begin{matrix} 2 \\ 2 \end{matrix} \end{matrix} \\ 3 \end{matrix}$

$54 < \begin{matrix} 9 < \begin{matrix} 3 \\ 3 \end{matrix} \\ 6 < \begin{matrix} 3 \\ 2 \end{matrix} \end{matrix}$

18

Solution 15

The factors of 36 are 1, 2, 3, 4, 6, 9, 12, 18, and 36.
The factors of 54 are 1, 2, 3, 6, 9, 18, 27, and 54.
The common factors of 36 and 54 are 1, 2, 3, 6, 9, and 18.
Among the numbers above that are common factors of both 36 and 54, 18 is the greatest common factor.

3.9: Common Multiples (of Two or More Numbers)

Definition: A number that is a multiple of all of the given numbers (multiples that are common to two or more numbers).
Examples:
Common multiples of 6 and 16: 48, 96, . . .
Common multiples of 12, 14, 15: 420, 840, . . .

Problem 16

Find the common multiples of 4 and 6.

12, 24, 36

Solution 16

Multiples of 4 are: 4, 8, 12, 16, 20, 24, 28, 32, 36 . . .
Multiples of 6 are: 6, 12, 18, 24, 30, 36, . . .
So, the common multiples of 4 and 6 are: 12, 24, 36, . . .

3.10: Least Common Multiple (LCM)

Definition: The smallest multiple of two (or more) numbers (the smallest number that is a multiple of both).

Examples:

LCM of 6 and 16 is 48

LCM of 12, 14, 15 is 420

Problem 17

Calculate the LCM of 3 and 4.

12

Solution 17

Multiples of 3: 3, 6, 9, (12) 15, 18, 21, (24) . . .
Multiples of 4: 4, 8, (12) 16, 20, (24) 28, . . .
The LCM of 3 and 4 is 12.

On Your Own Problem 4

Calculate the least positive integer that is divisible by 2, 3, 4, and 9.

36

3.11: Greatest Common Divisor (GCD)

Definition: The GCD of two or more integers is the largest integer that is a factor of each of them. Note that this term is similar to GCF. In addition, the same abbreviation is used for the Greatest Common Denominator, a concept necessary to add or subtract fractions.

Examples:

GCD of 12 and 18 is 6

GCD of 12 and 36 is 12

Problem 18

Calculate the GCD of two positive integers a and b, $a \geq b$.

Solution 18

Use Euclid's division algorithm:

Compute the remainder c of dividing a by b.

If the remainder c is zero, b is the greatest common divisor. If c is not zero, replace a with b and b with the remainder c. Go back to step (1).

For example, to solve this, try plugging in numbers for a and b, such as $a = 18$ and $b = 12$. Following the two-step approach shown above then leads you to compute the remainder c by dividing a by b:

$$18 \div 12 = 1 \text{ and } c = 6$$

$c = 6$, so you move to the next step and replace a with b and b with the remainder, or $a = 12$ and $b = c = 6$; $a \div b = 12 \div 6 = 2$

and (the new) $c = 0$,

thus GCD $= b = 6$

3.12: Prime Numbers

Definition: A prime number is a positive integer *greater* than 1 that is only divisible by the number 1 and by itself; in other words, it has *exactly* two whole number factors: itself and the number 1. Note that even though it is divisible by 1 and by itself, 1 is not a prime number.

Example: 2, 3, 5, 7, 11, 13, 17, 19, 23, 29, . . .

Problem 19

Two sides of a triangle are 6 and 20. Find a prime number that could be its third side.

$$6 + 20 > x$$
$$26 > x$$
$$x + 6 > 20$$
$$x > 14$$

$$14 < x < 26$$
$$17, 19, 23$$

Solution 19

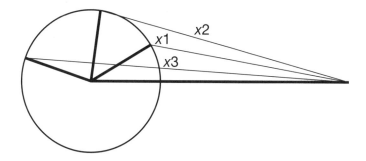

Let the third side of the triangle be x. In the figure above, three different lengths ($x1$, $x2$, $x3$) for x were shown to illustrate the fact that the range of its values is not only limited but also well defined.

The sum of the two sides of a triangle will always be greater than the third side ("$x1$, $x2$, $x3$" in the figure above). As a result, given a triangle with sides "6," "20," and "x," one can write the following inequalities:

$$6 + 20 > x \quad \text{or} \quad x < 26$$
$$x + 6 > 20 \quad \text{or} \quad x > 14$$
$$x + 20 > 6 \quad \text{or} \quad x > -14$$

Combining the above inequalities leads to
$$14 < x < 26$$

There are three prime numbers that satisfy the last double inequality. Any of the three is a correct answer: 17, 19, or 23

3.13: Ratio

Definition: Mathematical relationship between two quantities expressed as the quotient of those quantities.

Example: The ratio of a and b is $\frac{a}{b}$

Let $a = 6$ (dividend) and $b = 2$ (divisor) then

$\frac{a}{b} = a \div b = 6 \div 2 = 3$ (quotient)

Problem 20

The measures of the three angles in a triangle are in the ratio 1:2:6. Calculate their measures.

$$A + B + C = x + 2x + 6x = 9x = 180$$
$$x = 20$$
$$A = 20$$
$$B = 40$$
$$C = 120$$

Solution 20

Let the measures of the three angles be A, B, and C, and $A + B + C = 180°$. Given that $A:B:C$ is 1:2:6, it follows that A, B, C can be expressed as $x:2x:6x$

Consequently:
$$A + B + C = x + 2x + 6x = 9x = 180°$$
$$x = \frac{180°}{9} = 20°$$

Thus:
$$A = x = 20°$$
$$B = 2x = 40°$$
$$C = 6x = 120°$$

3.14: Percent

Definition: Percent (%) is a ratio in which the second quantity is the number 100. It is the number of hundredths or parts out of 100. Percentage means parts per 100 (i.e., a way of expressing a number as a fraction of 100).

Example: Percent is a ubiquitous concept in the math sections of the SAT. Although very few advanced students will ever mention it as a difficult topic, I found it to be not as trivial as one might think—probably because its widest usage in problem solving is prone to a straightforward application of the formula used to define it or a variation of it. The results, however, are usually a mixed bag, particularly when the concept is used in problems with a level of difficulty rated as "medium" or "hard." The following is an approach to a better understanding of this concept, emphasizing its roots and applicability.

For example, Johnny does a very good job working at McDonald's during his summer vacation, and after his first month, his boss tells him: "Congratulations, starting next month your monthly salary will increase by $150."

Sounds a little awkward, doesn't it? Wouldn't it sound more realistic if his boss were to say: "Congratulations, you just got yourself a 5% raise!"

What is the moral of this story?

Two different ways of expression were used to deliver the same message. The latter sounds more realistic, maybe because it is consistent with our perpetual quest to simplify the language we used in a casual/colloquial conversation.

We can use percentages to quantify the (percent of) change when a quantity goes up or down. Comparing the amount of change to the original amount gives us a simple method to compare quantities in general.

A common approach to solving problems using this concept is based on answering two questions:

Q1: Which are the two quantities to be compared?

Q2: Which one of the two quantities represents the reference (i.e., 100%)?

The above approach will be used to solve three SAT problems rated "easy," "medium," and "hard," respectively. By using the same methodology, the above qualifiers become irrelevant as the problems will seem almost identical in terms of their degree of difficulty.

Problem 21

What percent of 8 is 20?

$$\frac{8}{20} = \frac{100}{x} = 250\%$$

Solution 21

The answers to the two strategic questions (Q1 and Q2) above are:

A1: 8 and 20

A2: 8

A2 tells us that our reference is 8, therefore we are asked to compare 20 against 8. As such, we say that 8 represents 100% and 20 represents x%, and all we need to do is calculate x. The problem can be now set up in a manner that applies the concept of directly proportional numbers, for example:

8 . . . . 100%

20 . . . . x%

$$\frac{8}{20} = \frac{100}{x} \text{ or } x = \frac{2000}{8} = 250\%$$

The answer is 20 is/represents 250% of 8.

Problem 22

If a is 25% of b, then b is greater than a by what percent?

$$\frac{a}{b} = \frac{100}{x} = \frac{100b}{a} = x$$

$$a = \frac{25b}{100} = \frac{b}{4}$$

$$x = 100 \left(\frac{1}{4}\right)$$

$$x = 400\%$$

$$400 - 100 = 300$$

Solution 22

The answers to the two strategic questions (Q1 and Q2) above are:

A1: a and b

A2: a

A2 tells us that our reference is a, therefore we are asked to compare b against a. As such, we say that a represents 100% and b represents x% and all we need to do is calculate x. The problem can be now set up in a manner that applies the concept of directly proportional numbers:

$$a \ldots\ldots\ldots\ldots\ldots\ldots\ldots\ldots\ldots\ldots\ldots 100\%$$
$$b \ldots\ldots\ldots\ldots\ldots\ldots\ldots\ldots\ldots\ldots x\%$$

$$\frac{a}{b} = \frac{100}{x} \text{ or } x = \frac{100b}{a}\% \qquad \text{(Equation 1)}$$

In addition, the problem states that "a is 25% of b" or "$a = 25\%$ of b" or $a = \frac{25b}{100} = \frac{b}{4}$ (Equation 2)

Combining (Equation 1) and (Equation 2) by substituting $\frac{b}{4}$ for a in (1) leads to:

$$x = 100 \times \tfrac{1}{4} \text{ or } x = 400\%$$

Given that $a = 100\%$ and $b = 400\%$, the answer is the difference, or

b is greater than a by 300%

Problem 23

The stock price of a company fell by 20%. By how much does it have to rise to get back to the initial value?

$$.8s = 100 \qquad .8\frac{s}{s} = \frac{100}{y}$$
$$s = y$$

$$.8 = \frac{8}{10} = \frac{4}{5} = \frac{100}{y}$$

$$\frac{500}{4} = y = 125\%$$

$$125 - 100 = 25\%$$

Solution 23

We first need to identify the quantities to be compared using percents. Assume the initial value of the company's stock to be S. This value we were told dropped by 20%. As a result, the new value of the company's stock is $0.80 \times S$. This value will then have to go back up to the initial value: S.

The answers to the two strategic questions (Q1 and Q2) above are:

A1: $(0.80 \times S)$ and S

A2: $0.80 \times S$

A2 tells us that our reference is $0.80 \times S$, therefore we are asked to compare S against $0.80 \times S$. As such, we say that $0.80 \times S$ represents 100% and S represents y% and all we need to do is calculate y. The problem can be now set up in a manner that applies the concept of directly proportional numbers:

$$0.80 \times S \dots \dots \dots \dots \dots \dots \dots 100\%$$
$$S \dots \dots \dots \dots \dots \dots \dots \dots \dots \dots y\%$$

$$0.80 \times \frac{S}{S} = \frac{100}{y}$$

or

$$\frac{0.80 \times S}{S} = 0.80 = \frac{8}{10} = \frac{4}{5} = \frac{100}{y}$$

Thus:

$$y = \frac{5 \times 100}{4} = 125[\%]$$

We showed that if $0.80 \times S = 100\%$ then $S = 125\%$ and thus we calculated that S is greater than $0.80 \times S$ by the difference: 25%. Therefore, to get back to the original value, the stock will have to rise by 25%.

On Your Own Problem 5

The distribution of the number of years of higher education for a group of 8,000 adults is shown in the graph below. Calculate the number of adults with 6 or more years of higher education.

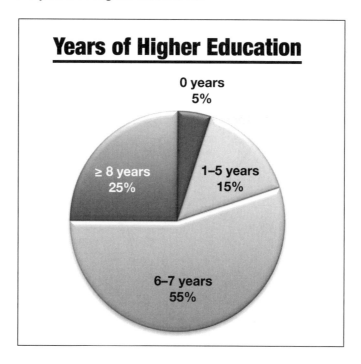

Years of Higher Education

0 years
5%

≥ 8 years
25%

1–5 years
15%

6–7 years
55%

$$\frac{x}{8000} \quad \frac{80}{100} = 100x = 640,000$$

$$x = 6,400$$

3.15: Proportion

Definition: Proportion is an equation in which two ratios are set equal to each other.

Examples:

$$\frac{a}{b} = \frac{x}{y}$$

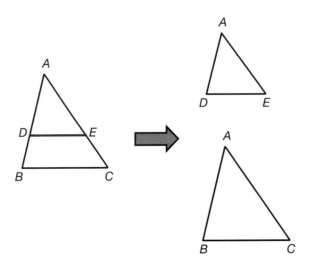

If $\triangle ADE$ and $\triangle ABC$ are similar, then

$$\frac{AD}{AB} = \frac{AE}{AC} = \frac{DE}{BC}$$

Also see Problems 72 and 103 for more on proportion.

3.16: Directly Proportional Quantities

Definition: Quantities in which ratios are constant; in other words, if one increases, the ones "directly proportional" with it also will increase. This also can be defined as quantities related such that if one increases, the other also will increase proportionally.

Example:

If quantities expressed by the values A and B are directly proportional,

$$\frac{A}{B} = \text{constant}$$

(A and B are directly proportional if $B = kA$ where k is a constant)

See topic below for sample problems.

3.17: Inversely Proportional Quantities

Definition: Quantities in which the product is constant; in other words, if one increases, the ones "inversely" proportional with it will decrease. This also can be defined as quantities related such that if one increases, the other will decrease proportionally.

Example:

If quantities expressed by the values A and B are inversely proportional,

$$A \times B = \text{constant}$$

(A and B are inversely proportional if $B = \dfrac{k}{A}$ where k is a constant)

Problem 24

John needs 20 days to paint a house. George works twice as fast as John. The two painters, John and George, work together for 2 days. After that, George had to work on a different project, and John continued to work by himself for another 3 days after which time he was reassigned to another project while George was asked to return to this work site. How many days will George need to complete the work?

$$G = 20 \quad J = 10$$

$$\frac{2}{20} + \frac{2}{10} + \frac{3}{20} = \frac{1}{10} + \frac{2}{10} = \frac{3}{10} + \frac{3}{20} = \frac{9}{20}$$

$$1 - \frac{9}{20} = \frac{11}{20} \qquad \frac{11}{20} \div \frac{1}{10} = 5.5$$

Solution 24

If John needs 20 days to paint the house and George works twice as fast than John, then George will only need 10 days to finish the same paint job.

Given the direct proportionality between the number of days worked and the ratio of work being done vs. total work, in one day, John and George will complete ½0 and ⅒ of the work, respectively. Working together for 2 days, they will paint twice as much and this leads to:

$$\frac{2}{20} + \frac{2}{10} = \frac{1}{10} + \frac{2}{10} = \frac{3}{10}$$

of the total work. Working alone for another 3 days, John will contribute another ³⁄₂₀ of work for a total of

$$\frac{3}{10} + \frac{3}{20} = \frac{9}{20}$$

of the work needed. That means that George was left to complete the remaining

$$1 - \frac{9}{20} = \frac{11}{20}$$

of the total work. Given that he can paint $\frac{1}{10}$ of the house in one day, the number of days he will need to complete the work is

$$\frac{11}{20} \div \frac{1}{10} = 5.5 \ [days]$$

Also see Problem 8 for more on direct and inverse proportions.

3.18: Sequence

Definition: Ordered, finite/infinite list of numbers/terms (usually following a specific pattern), separated by commas.
Examples:
First term = -3; every term thereafter is obtained by adding 5, or
-3, 2, 7, 12, 17, . . .
First term is 5; every term thereafter is obtained by multiplying the previous one by 3, or
5, 15, 45, 135, . . .

In general, if one has a sequence (an arithmetic sequence; see Section 3.19) of N consecutive numbers of which the first and the last ones are known, one can find their sum by using the formula: Sum = N(First Number + Last Number)/2

Note: The derivation is quite simple if you pair up the first and the last, the second and the one before last, and so forth, and you notice that the sum of each pair is the same. Thus, the total sum is the sum of a pair multiplied by the number of pairs ($N/2$).

Problem 25

Calculate the sum of all integers from 1 to 100 without using a calculator.

$$\frac{100\,(1+100)}{2} = 50 \times 101 = 5050$$

Solution 25

$$\text{Sum} = \frac{100(1+100)}{2} = 50 \times 101 = 5050$$

3.19: Arithmetic Sequence

Definition: Sequence in which the difference between any two consecutive terms is the same (i.e., d in the example below).

Example: 2, 7, 12, 17, . . . where $d = 7 - 2 = 12 - 7 = 17 - 12 =$

Given an arithmetic sequence:

$$a_1, a_2, a_3, \ldots\ldots\ldots\ldots a_n$$

by definition, a general term k is equal to the previous term $(k - 1) + d$, or

$$a_k = a_{k-1} + d$$

The relationship between term n and the first term of the sequence is:

$$a_2 = a_1 + d = a_1 + 1d$$
$$a_3 = a_2 + d = a_1 + 2d$$
$$a_4 = a_3 + d = a_1 + 3d$$
$$a_n = a_1 + (n - 1)d$$

Problem 26

The first term of a sequence of numbers is −4. Every term thereafter is obtained by adding 5. What is the value of the 401st term of the sequence?

(A) 1996
(B) 2005
(C) 1999
(D) 2001

$$-4 + 5(n-1)$$
$$-4 + 5(401-1) = 1996$$

Solution 26

In general, problems with sequences (arithmetic or geometric) require calculation of a higher ranked term given that the first term is known and so is the formula for subsequent terms.

Applying the formula that calculates the "next term" and working your way up to the required term, one term at a time is *not* recommended. (Keep in mind that this is a timed test in which you have on average a little more than a minute to solve a problem.)

The *recommended* solution will have to be based on a way to identify a pattern for the calculation of a general term and extrapolate it to the rank in question.

Solution A

To solve the problem as it is presented to us (i.e., as a multiple-choice problem), writing a few terms should help us discover the pattern. The results are captured in the table below.

Rank	Term
1	−4
2	1
3	6
4	11
5	16
…	…
401	?

Looking at the above results should provide enough ammunition to our observational skills to notice that all odd terms end in 6 (except for the first one) and even terms in 1. Thus, given that 401 is an odd rank, the corresponding term will have to end in 6. The only answer that ends in 6 is 1996 and as a result, the correct answer is A.

Solution B

I will present next a more general method to solve this problem. Although this method will require more time than the one presented as Solution A, it has the merit of solving this and similar problems in a generic and a more general way, including instances where they are given in the open-ended format.

Rank	Term (formula)
1	−4
2	$-4 + 5 \times 1$
3	$-4 + 5 \times 2$
4	$-4 + 5 \times 3$
5	$-4 + 5 \times 4$
…	…
N	?

By observation, the formula for the Nth rank is:

$$-4 + 5 \times (n - 1)$$

When $N = 401$, the above formula allows us to calculate the 401st term, or

$$-4 + 5 \times (401 - 1) = -4 + 2000 = 1996$$

The correct result is A.

3.20: Geometric Sequence

Definition: Sequence in which the ratio between any two consecutive terms is the same (i.e., r in the example below).

Example:

$$3, 6, 12, 24, 48, \ldots$$

$$r = \frac{6}{3} = \frac{12}{6} = \frac{24}{12} = \ldots = 2$$

In general, given a geometric sequence

$$a_1, a_2, a_3, \ldots\ldots\ldots a_n$$

by definition, a general term k is equal with the previous term $(k - 1)$ multiplied by r, or

$$a_k = (a_{k-1})r$$

The relationship between term n and the first term of the sequence is:

$$a_n = a_1(r^{n-1})$$

Problem 27

The first term of a sequence is 5. Every term thereafter is obtained by multiplying the previous one by 3. What is the value of the 5th term of the sequence?

$$5 \cdot 3^{5-1} = 405$$

Solution 27

$n = 5$

the 5th term $= 5 \times 3^{5-1} = 405$

On Your Own Problem 6

$$m, n, 48, \ldots$$

In the sequence above, the first term is m and each term thereafter is twice the preceding term. Calculate the value of $(m + n)$.

$$48 / 2 = 24$$
$$24 / 2 = 12 \quad +$$
$$\overline{\qquad}$$
$$36$$

On Your Own Problem 7

$$3, 9, 27, \ldots$$

In the sequence shown above, the first term is 3, and each term thereafter is three times the preceding term—making this a geometric sequence. Calculate the kth term of the sequence.

$$3^k$$

On Your Own Problem 8

$$300, 150, 75, 226, 113, 340, 170, \ldots$$

Calculate the 10th term of the sequence above given that its first term is 300 and each term thereafter is obtained (1) dividing the previous term by 2, if the previous term is even, or (2) multiplying the previous term by 3 and then adding 1, if the previous term is odd.

$$85, 256, \boxed{128}$$

On Your Own Problem 9

Consider a geometric sequence of positive numbers. After the first term, the ratio of each term to the term immediately preceding it is 3 to 1. Calculate the ratio of the 9th term in this sequence to the 6th term.

$$3^6 = 729$$
$$3^9 = 19683 \qquad 27:1$$

3.21: Set

Definition: Collection of things referred to as "elements" or "members" of the set.
Examples:
set A = {1, 3, 5, 7, 9}
set B = {3, 9, 10, 11}

Problem 28

Write the set of numbers that do not belong to the domain (see Section 4.9) of the function.

$$f(x) = \frac{2x}{(x-1)(x-3)(x+5)}$$

$-5, 1, 3$

Solution 28

These are the values of x for which the denominator of $f(x)$ is equal to 0, or

$$x \in \{-5, 1, 3\}$$

3.22: Union

Definition: Set that includes all elements of the sets entering the union.
Examples:
The union of two sets A and B, written $A \cup B$, is the set of elements that are either in set A, set B, or both. For sets A and B defined in Section 3.21, their union is therefore

$A \cup B = \{1, 3, 5, 7, 9, 10, 11\}$

The union of A and B is represented by the shaded area in the diagram shown below.

3.23: Intersection

Definition: A set that includes only the elements that the sets entering the union have in common.
Example: The intersection of two sets A and B, written $A \cap B$, is the set of elements which are in both A and B.

$A \cap B = \{3, 9\}$

The intersection of A and B is represented by the shaded area in the diagram shown below.

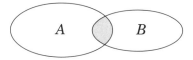

3.24: Venn Diagram

Definition: Diagrams that show all possible logical relations between a finite (in SAT problems, two, maximum three) collections of sets.

Example:

A Venn diagram uses overlapping circles/ovals to show relationships between groups of objects.

In this example, sets A, B, and C have common elements.

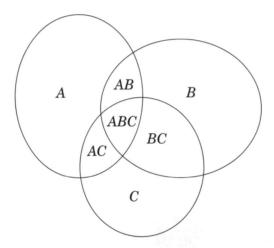

Problem 29

In a high school class, it is mandatory for all students to belong to a language club. The languages offered are Spanish and Russian. S students are enrolled in a Spanish club, R students in a Russian club, and C students are enrolled in both. What is the ratio between students enrolled in the Spanish club but not in the Russian club and the total student population?

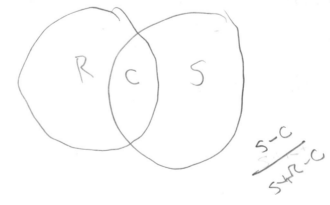

Solution 29

The Venn diagram describing the above problem is:

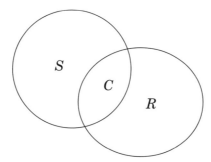

The requested ratio is:

$$\frac{S-C}{S+R-C}$$

3.25: Factorials

Definition: The factorial of n is the number of ways in which the n elements of a group can be ordered.

Example: The factorial of a number n represented by $n!$ is the product of the natural numbers up to and including n: $n! = 1 \times 2 \times \ldots \times (n-2) \times (n-1) \times n$

Problem 30

A cafeteria has a lunch special consisting of soup or salad; a sandwich; coffee, tea, or a nonalcoholic beverage; and a dessert. If the menu lists 2 soups, 3 salads, 6 sandwiches, and 10 desserts, how many different lunches can one choose?

$(2+3) \cdot 6 \cdot (1+1+1) \cdot 10 = 900$

Solution 30

The group of four elements the combinations of which we need to calculate (see also Section 3.27) is:

soup/salad, sandwich, coffee/tea/beverage, dessert

The corresponding numbers involved in the combinations are:

2/3, 6, 1/1/1, 10

The number of different lunches is:

$$(2 + 3) \times 6 \times (1 + 1 + 1) \times 10 = 5 \times 6 \times 3 \times 10 = 900$$

3.26: Permutation

Definition: A possible selection of a certain number of objects taken from a group with regard to order. (The number of ways a given set of things can be arranged, where order is considered to make a difference.)

Example: The permutation $n\,\mathrm{P}_r$ is the number of subgroups of size r that can be taken from a set with n elements. It is calculated as follows:

$$n\,\mathrm{P}_r = \frac{n!}{(n-r)!}$$

Problem 31

Calculate the permutations (i.e., total number of combinations) of two letters that can be formed from a group of three letters: A, B, C.

$$\frac{3!}{(3-2)!} = 6$$

Solution 31

The number of permutations is:

$$3P_2 = \frac{3!}{(3-2)!} = \frac{6}{1} = 6$$

and the groups are:

AB, AC, BC, BA, CA, CB

3.27: Combination

Definition: A possible selection of a certain number of objects taken from a group without regard to order.

Example: Combinations is the number of unordered subgroups of size r that are selected from a set of size n. It is calculated as follows:

$$nC_r = \frac{nP_r}{r!} = \frac{n!}{r!(n-r)!}$$

Note that the difference between permutations and combinations consists in the fact that subgroups selected from a given set are ordered and unordered, respectively.

Problem 32

How many combinations of two letters can be formed from a set of three letters: A, B, and C?

$$\frac{3!}{2!\,(3-2)!} = 3$$

Solution 32

The number of combinations is given by:

$$3C_2 = \frac{3P_2}{2!} = \frac{3!}{2!(3-2)!} = 3$$

and the groups are:

AB, AC, BC

The order in which we wrote the letters is of no concern; that is, AB could be written BA, but we would still have only one combination of the letters A and B.

On Your Own Problem 10

An ice cream shop offers 5 different toppings for its ice cream cakes. The regular/standard price includes 2 different combinations. Calculate how many different combinations of toppings are available for no additional cost.

$$\frac{5!}{2!(5-2)!} = 10$$

3.28: Absolute Value

Definition: The absolute value of a number a, denoted as $|a|$, is the distance (i.e., *always* a positive number) between a and 0 on the number line.

Examples:

$|a| = a$; if $a > 0$

$|a| = 0$; if $a = 0$

$|a| = -a$; if $a < 0$

$|8| = 8$ and $|-8| = 8$

Absolute Value Inequality

Example: Demonstrate that if $|x - a| \leq b$ then $a - b \leq x \leq a + b$

Solution:

By definition, $|x - a| =$

    1) $x - a$ if $x - a \geq 0$ or $x \geq a$

    2) $-x + a$ if $x - a < 0$ or $x < a$

Case 1:

    If $x \geq a$

    then $|x - a| = x - a \leq b$ or $x \leq a + b$

    and the intersection of the two intervals is

    $x \geq a \cap x \leq a + b$ or $a \leq x \leq a + b$

Case 2:

    If $x < a$

    then $|x - a| = a - x \leq b$ or $x \geq a - b$

    and the intersection of the two intervals is

    $x < a \cap x \geq a - b$ or $a - b \leq x < a$

The union of the results of 1 and 2 gives us the solution:

    $a \leq x \leq a + b \cup a - b \leq x < a$ or

    $a - b \leq x \leq a + b$

Problem 33

Simplify $| 2 + 3(-4) |$

$$|2 + -12|$$
$$|-10|$$
$$10$$

Solution 33

$| 2 + 3(-4) | = | 2 - 12 | = | -10 | = 10$

Problem 34

Simplify $-|-4|$

-4

Solution 34

$-|-4| = -(4) = -4$

Problem 35

Simplify $-|(-2)^2|$

-4

Solution 35

$-|(-2)^2| = -|4| = -4$

Problem 36

Simplify $-|-2|^2$

-4

Solution 36

$-|-2|^2 = -(2)^2 = -(4) = -4$

Problem 37

Simplify $(-|-2|)^2$

4

Solution 37

$(-|-2|)^2 = (-(2))^2 = (-2)^2 = 4$

Chapter 4

Algebra

It isn't what people think that's important,
but the reason they think what they think.

—Eugène Ionesco

4.1: Monomial

Definition: Any number or variable or product of numbers and variables.

Examples: 3, $-4x$, xy^3, $1.5xy^2a^3b^4$

Problem 38

Find the product

$$(3a^2b^3)(-2a^5b^2)$$

$$-6a^7b^5$$

Solution 38

$$(3a^2b^3)(-2a^5b^2) = -6a^7b^5$$

Remember your exponential formulas/rules:

$a^b \times a^c = a^{b+c}$

$(a^b)^c = a^{bc}$

$a^b/a^c = a^{b-c}$

4.2: Coefficient

Definition: The number that appears in front of the variable(s).

Example: Given monomials $2a$; $-3xy$; and $17x^2yz^5$, their corresponding coefficients are 2, -3, and 17.

Problem 39

Calculate the coefficient of

$$2a \times (-3xy) \times 17x^2yz^5$$

$$-102ax^3y^2z^5$$

Solution 39

The resulting monomial is:

$$-102ax^3y^2z^5$$

and its coefficient is -102.

4.3: Polynomial

Definition: A polynomial is the sum of two or more monomials.
Example: $xy^3 + 1.5xy^2a^3b^4$

Problem 40

Find the product

$$-5b(2b^5 + 7b^3 - 9b)$$

(handwritten) $-10b^6 - 35b^4 + 45b^2$

Solution 40

$$-5b(2b^5 + 7b^3 - 9b) =$$
$$-5b(2b^5) - 5b(7b^3) - 5b(-9b) =$$
$$-10b^6 - 35b^4 + 45b^2$$

4.4: Term

Definition: The term (of a polynomial) is each monomial that makes up the polynomial (i.e., a number, a variable, or a product of a number and a variable or variables).

Example:
binomials = polynomials with two terms (e.g., $5x - 10$)
trinomials = polynomials with three terms (e.g., $7x^3 + 2x - 4$)

The degree of a term is the sum of the exponents on the variables contained in the term.

Problem 41

Calculate the degrees of $2ab$ and $5y^3$

$$3$$

Solution 41

The degree of the term $2ab$ is $1 + 1 = 2$. The exponent on a is 1 and on b is 1 and the sum of the exponents is 2.

The degree of the term $5y^3$ would be 3 because the exponent of the only variable contained in the term is 3.

4.5: Like Terms

Definition: Terms that have exactly the same variables and exponents; they are the only terms of the polynomial that can be combined.
Example: $5a^2b^3$ and $-13a^2b^3$

Problem 42

Calculate the coefficients a, b, c, and d such that

$$ax^3 + bx^2 + cx + d = (x - 1)(x + 1)(2x + 3)$$

$$(x^2-1)(2x+3)$$

$$2x^3 - 2x + 3x^2 - 3$$

$$2x^3 + 3x^2 - 2x - 3$$

Solution 42

$$(x - 1)(x + 1)(2x + 3) = (x^2 - 1)(2x + 3) =$$
$$2x^3 - 2x + 3x^2 - 3 =$$
$$2x^3 + 3x^2 - 2x - 3 =$$

Thus,

$$a = 2, b = 3, c = -2, d = -3$$

4.6: Exponents

Definition: Exponents are shorthand for multiplication: $(5)(5) = 5^2$, $(5)(5)(5) = 5^3$. The exponent stands for however many times the number, variable, or a combination (product) of the two are being multiplied. The quantity that's being multiplied is called the *base*. This process of using exponents is called *raising to a power*, where the exponent is the "power." So, 5^3 is "five, raised to the third power." When we deal with numbers, we usually just simplify; we'd rather deal with 27 than with 3^3. But with variables, we need the exponents, because we'd rather deal with A^6 than with $A \times A \times A \times A \times A \times A$.

Properties.
$$(x^m)(x^n) = x^{(m + n)}$$
$$(x^m)^n = x^{mn}$$

Any number that is not 0 raised to the power 0 is just 1. As a result,

$$x^{-n} = \frac{1}{x^n}$$

Example: Write $\left(\dfrac{x^{-2}}{y^{-3}}\right)^{-2}$ using only positive exponents.

$$\left(\frac{x^{-2}}{y^{-3}}\right)^{-2} = \frac{x^{(-2)(-2)}}{y^{(-3)(-2)}} = \frac{x^4}{y^6}$$

Problem 43

Given the following equation

$$64^{x-3} = 2^{-3x}$$

Calculate x.

[Handwritten:]

$64 = 8 \cdot 8 = 2^3 \cdot 2^3 = 2^6$

$\left(2^6\right)^{x-3} = 2^{-3x}$

$2^{6(x-3)} = 2^{-3x}$

$6(x-3) = -3x$

$9x = 18$

$x = 2$

Solution 43

$$64 = 8 \times 8 = 2^3 \times 2^3 = 2^6$$

Thus $(2^6)^{x-3} = 2^{-3x}$
$2^{6(x-3)} = 2^{-3x}$
$6(x-3) = -3x$
$9x = 18$
$x = 2$

4.7: Function

Definition: Rule/formula describing how to associate elements that belong to two different sets ("domain" and "range," see below); it assigns to each number in one set (domain) a number in the other set (range).

Examples:

Example #1:

$$f(x) = \frac{8}{x(x-3)}$$

where x = "argument" (of the function)

Example #2:

$$f(x) = \sqrt{x - 7}$$

The graphical representation of the function $y = f(x)$ in the xy coordinate system for the two examples above is shown below:

Example #1:

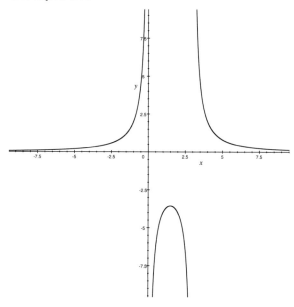

Example #2:

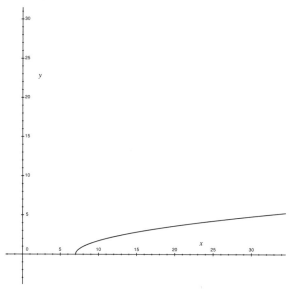

4.8: Quadratic Function

Definition: Polynomial function that takes the form: $ax^2 + bx + c$ where $a \neq 0$ (the highest exponent of x is 2); its graph is a second degree polynomial or a parabola (see graph example below).

Example:

$f(x) = ax^2 + bx + c = 0$

Solution: $x_{1,2} = \dfrac{-b \pm \sqrt{b^2 - 4ac}}{2a}$

where: $f(x) = a(x - x_1)(x - x_2)$

The graph of a quadratic function is a parabola:

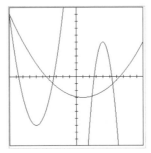

Problem 44

A rancher has 1200 meters of fence to enclose a rectangular corral with another fence dividing it in the middle as in the diagram below.

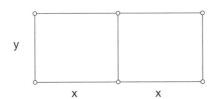

Calculate the largest possible area that can be enclosed with the available fence.

$4x + 3y = 1200$

$3y = 1200 - 4x$

$y = \dfrac{1200 - 4x}{3}$

$A = 2xy$

$2x(400 - 4x/3)$

$x = 0, 300$

Solution 44

Total area: $A = 2xy$

In addition, x and y must satisfy.

$$3y + 4x = 1200$$
$$3y = 1200 - 4x$$
$$y = 400 - 4x/3$$

We now have y expressed as a function of x, and we can substitute this expression for y in the formula for total area A.

$$A = 2xy = 2x\,(400 - 4x/3)$$

We need to find the value of x that makes A as large as possible. A is a quadratic function of x, and the graph opens downward, so the highest point on the graph of A is the vertex. The graph of the function (not required to solve the problem) is shown below:

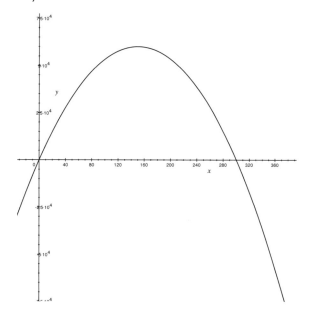

Because A is factored, the easiest way to find the vertex is to find the x-intercepts and average.

$$2x\,(400 - 4x/3) = 0$$
$$2x = 0 \text{ or } 400 - 4x/3 = 0$$
$$x = 0 \text{ or } 400 = 4x/3$$
$$x = 0 \text{ or } 1200 = 4x$$
$$x = 0 \text{ or } 300 = x$$

Therefore, the line of symmetry of the graph of A is x = 150, the average of 0 and 300.

Now that we know the value of x corresponding to the largest area, we can find the value of y by going back to the equation relating x and y.

$$y = 400 - \frac{4x}{3} = 400 - \frac{4(150)}{3} = 200$$

The maximum value of the area A is therefore

$$A_{max} = 2 \times 150 \times 200 = 60,000 \ [m^2]$$

4.9: Domain

Definition: The domain of a function is the set of all of the values for which the function is defined (the x values).

Example: The domains of the functions illustrated in the two examples in the function section above are:

Example #1:

$$f(x) = \frac{8}{x(x-3)}$$

Domain:

$x \in (-\infty, 0) \cap (0,3) \cap (3, +\infty)$ or $x \in (-\infty, +\infty) - \{0,3\}$

Example #2:

$$f(x) = \sqrt{x-7}$$

Domain:

$x \geq 7$ or $x \in [7, +\infty)$

Example #3:

$f(x) = x^2 - 2x + 5$

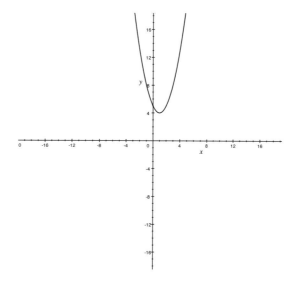

Example #4:

$f(x) = \dfrac{x + 4}{x - 2}$

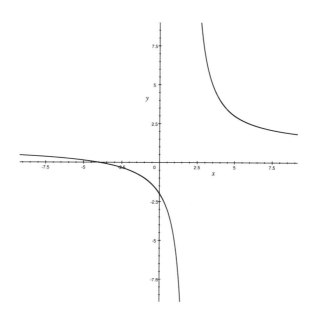

Example #5:

$f(x) = \sqrt{x+5}$

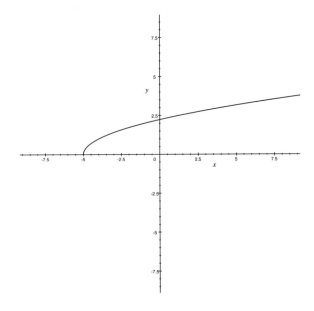

The domains for the three functions shown above are

Function	Domain
$f(x) = x^2 - 2x + 5$	$(-\infty, +\infty)$
$f(x) = \dfrac{x+4}{x-2}$	$(-\infty, 2) \cup (2, +\infty)$
$f(x) = \sqrt{x+5}$	$[-5, +\infty)$

4.10: Range

Definition: Range (of a function) is the set of all of the values that are the output (result) of applying the function (the *f(x)* or *y* values).

Example:

The range of values for *f(x)* corresponding to each interval on which *x* is defined in the graphs shown in the domain section is shown below.

Function	Range
$f(x) = \dfrac{8}{x(x-3)}$	$\left(-\infty, -\dfrac{32}{9}\right) \cup (0, +\infty)$
$f(x) = \sqrt{x-7}$	$[0, +\infty)$
$f(x) = x^2 - 2x + 5$	$[4, +\infty)$
$f(x) = \dfrac{x+4}{x-2}$	$(-\infty, +\infty)$

Function	Range
$f(x) = \sqrt{x+5}$	$[0, +\infty)$

4.11: Interpreting and Solving Equations/Inequalities

Systems of (linear) equations can be solved using techniques such as substitution, elimination/addition, graphing, and Gaussian elimination. The most popular ones are substitution (see Problem 4) and elimination/addition (see Problem 3).

In solving inequalities or systems of inequalities, most rules and properties used to solve linear equations/systems of equations are valid. A notable exception is the following:

If the signs of both sides of an inequality are changed (or both sides are multiplied by a negative number), then the sense of the inequality will change, so if

$$x < y$$

then

$$-x > -y$$

Problem 45

As a technician with a small computer repair company, James is assigned a certain number of computers that need repair per week. The equation is:

$$C = 20 - 4d$$

where C = number of computers left for repair (from the week's allotment) at the end of each day and d = number of days he has worked that week. In the equation above, explain the meaning of the value 20.

(A) James repairs computers at a rate of 20 per day.

(B) James will complete the repairs within 20 days.

(C) James repairs computers at a rate of 20 per hour.

(D) James starts each week with the goal of repairing 20 computers by week's end.

Solution 45

When $d = 0$ (i.e., James starts his first day of that week), $C = 20$. Therefore, the correct answer is C. See also Problems 190 and 195 for more sample problems.

On Your Own Problem 11

$$60 < \frac{2x-1}{4} < 61$$

If $y = \frac{2x+1}{2}$, given the double inequality shown above, calculate one possible integer value of y.

$241/2 = 122$

4.12: Cartesian Coordinate System

Definition: The Cartesian coordinate system, or rectangular coordinate system, is used to determine each point uniquely in a plane through two numbers, usually called the x-coordinate and the y-coordinate of the point. To define the coordinates, two perpendicular directed lines (the x-axis or abscissa, and the y-axis or ordinate), are specified, as well as the unit length, which is marked off on the two axes.

Example:

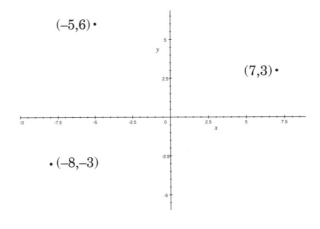

See Problems 46, 47, 61, 72, 73, 80, and 203 for sample problems using this system.

4.13: Straight Line

Definition: Lines in a Cartesian plane can be described algebraically by linear equations and linear functions. In two dimensions, the characteristic equation is often given in the slope-intercept form:

$$y = mx + b$$

where:

m is the slope of the line (see below)

b is the y-intercept of the line

x is the independent variable of the function y

Example:

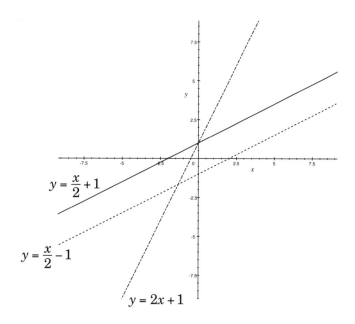

See Problems 46, 47, 80, and 187 for sample problems.

4.14: Slope

Definition: One of the most important properties of straight lines is their angle from the horizontal plane. This concept is called *slope*.

Examples: Consider points A and B of coordinates (x_1, y_1) and (x_2, y_2), respectively. By definition, the slope of the line passing though A and B is

$$m = \frac{y_1 - y_2}{x_1 - x_2}$$

If two lines of slopes m_1 and m_2, respectively, are perpendicular to each other,

$$m_1 \times m_2 = -1$$

If the two lines are parallel to each other,

$$m_1 = m_2$$

See Problems 46, 47, 80, and 146 for sample problems.

On Your Own Problem 12

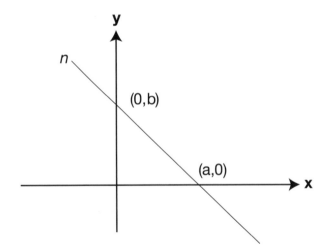

Calculate the slope of line *n* shown in the figure above.

$$\frac{b - 0}{0 - a} = m$$

$$\frac{-b}{a} = m$$

4.15: Distance

Definition: Let d be the distance from point A (x_1, y_1) to point B (x_2, y_2). (AB is a line segment.)
Example:

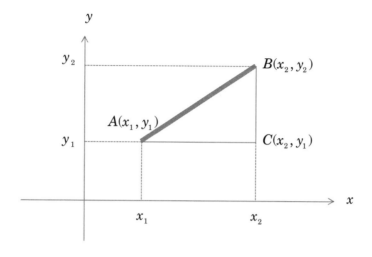

In the figure above, the Pythagorean Theorem gives us a relationship among the hypotenuse and the other two sides of the triangle $\triangle ABC$, so that

$$AB^2 = d^2 = AC^2 + BC^2 = (x_2 - x_1)^2 + (y_2 - y_1)^2$$

The formula for the distance is therefore:

$$d = \sqrt{(x_2 - x_1)^2 + (y_2 - y_1)^2}$$

See Problem 61 for a sample problem.

4.16: Midpoint

Definition: The midpoint is the point that divides a line segment into two segments of equal length.
Example: If $AM = BM$ then M = midpoint. In general, if the coordinates of A and B are (x_1, y_1) and (x_2, y_2), respectively, the coordinates of M are

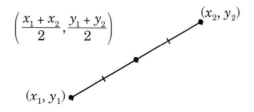

Problem 46

Rectangle *ABCD* lies in the *xy*-coordinate plane so that its sides are not parallel to the axes. What is the product of the slopes of all four sides of rectangle *ABCD*?

Solution 46

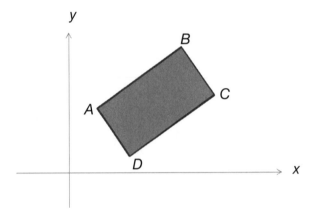

Let the slopes of the four sides of the rectangle *ABCD* be
$$m_1, m_2, m_3, m_4$$
Using the property of slopes of perpendicular lines, it follows that
$$m_1 \times m_2 = -1$$
$$m_3 \times m_4 = -1$$

Consequently,
$$m_1 \times m_2 \times m_3 \times m_4 = 1$$

Problem 47

In the *xy*-coordinate plane, the graph

$$x = y^2 - 9$$

intersects line *l* at (0, *a*) and (7, *b*). What is the greatest slope of *l*?

$$\frac{4 - (-3)}{7} = 1 \qquad \begin{array}{l} 0 = a^2 - 9 \\ 7 = b^2 - 9 \end{array} \qquad \begin{array}{l} a^2 = 9 \\ a = \pm 3 \\ 16 = b^2 \\ b = \pm 4 \end{array}$$

Solution 47

First, we calculate *a* and *b* taking into account the fact that the two points, (0, *a*) and (7, *b*), satisfy the equation of the graph, or

$$0 = a^2 - 9$$
$$7 = b^2 - 9$$

Solving for *a* and *b* results in

$$a = \pm 3$$
$$b = \pm 4$$

The slope of *l* is given by

$$m = \frac{b - a}{7 - 0}$$

To obtain the greatest value of the slope one needs to maximize the above expression,

$$m_{MAX} = \frac{b_{MAX} - a_{MIN}}{7}$$

or, from the values of *a* and *b* calculated above,

$$m_{MAX} = \frac{4 - (-3)}{7} = \frac{7}{7} = 1$$

Problem 48

Find the value of p so that $(-2, 2.5)$ is the midpoint between $(p, 2)$ and $(-1, 3)$.

$$p = -3$$

Solution 48

$$\left(\frac{p + (-1)}{2}, \frac{2 + 3}{2} \right) = (-2, 2.5)$$

$$\left(\frac{p - 1}{2}, \frac{5}{2} \right) = (-2, 2.5)$$

$$\left(\frac{p - 1}{2}, 2.5 \right) = (-2, 2.5)$$

This reduces to needing to figure out what p is, in order to make the x-values work:

$$\frac{p - 1}{2} = -2$$

$$p - 1 = -4$$

$$p = -3$$

So the answer is

$$p = -3$$

On Your Own Problem 13

C is the midpoint of line segment AE, and B is the midpoint of line segment $\overline{AC}$. If D is a point located between C and E such that the length of the line segment $\overline{BD}$ is 20 and the length of the line segment $\overline{AD}$ is 39, calculate the length of the line segment $\overline{DE}$.

4.17: Complex Numbers

Definitions:

The Unit Imaginary Number:

$$i = \sqrt{-1}$$

or $i^2 = -1$; $i^3 = -i$; $i^4 = 1$, etc.

The Standard Form:

$$a + bi$$

where a and b are real numbers also referred to as real and imaginary parts, respectively.

The Conjugate of an Imaginary Number $(a + bi)$:

$$a - bi$$

Complex Arithmetic:

$$a + bi = 0 \text{ if and only if } a = b = 0$$
$$(a + bi) + (c + di) = (a + c) + (b + d)i$$
$$(a + bi)(c + di) = (ac - bd) + (bc + ad)i$$
$$(a + bi)(a - bi) = a2 + b2$$

Problem 49

$$\frac{a + bi}{c + di} = x + yi$$

Express x and y in terms of a, b, c, and d.

Solution 49

$$\frac{c-di}{c-di} \times \frac{a+bi}{c+di} = \frac{(ac+bd)+(bc-ad)i}{c^2+d^2} = \frac{ac+bd}{c^2+d^2} + \frac{bc-ad}{c^2+d^2}i = x+yi$$

or

$$x = \frac{ac+bd}{c^2+d^2}$$

$$y = \frac{bc-ad}{c^2+d^2}$$

Problem 50

If $\frac{5-2i}{4-3i} = x+yi$, calculate x and y.

Solution 50

$$\frac{5-2i}{4-3i} = \frac{(4+3i)(5-2i)}{(4+3i)(4-3i)} = \frac{20-8i+15i+6}{16+9} = \frac{26+7i}{25}$$

or

$$x = \frac{26}{25} \quad \text{and} \quad y = \frac{7}{25}$$

Problem 51

Simplify the following expression:

$$(3 - 2i) + (4 - 5i)(5 - 6i)$$

Solution 51

$$3 - 2i + 20 - 24i - 25i + 30 = 53 - 51i$$

Problem 52

Write the following complex expression in standard format:

$$\frac{5}{1 - 2i}$$

Solution 52

$$\frac{5}{1 - 2i} = \frac{5(1 + 2i)}{(1 + 2i)(1 - 2i)} = \frac{5 + 10i}{1 + 4} = 1 + 2i$$

Chapter 5

Geometry

It's not that I'm so smart, it's just that I stay with problems longer.

—Albert Einstein

5.1: Angles

Definition: An angle is a shape formed by two lines/rays ("the legs") diverging from a common point ("the vertex").

Example: The intersection of two line segments, *AB* and *BC*:

See Problems 54, 55, 57, 67, 69, 71, 73, and 192 for sample problems.

5.2: Vertex

Definition: The point of intersection or the common point at which two lines/rays are joined.

Example:

See Problems 54, 55, 57, 67, 69, 71, 73, and 192 for sample problems.

5.3: Acute Angles

Definition: An angle that measures < 90°.
Example:

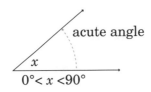

See Problems 54, 55, 73, and 192 for sample problems.

5.4: Obtuse Angles

Definition: An angle that measures > 90° but < 180°.
Example:

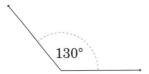

See problems 53, 67, and 192 for sample problems.

Useful Definitions/Properties of Angles

Alternate Interior Angles

For any pair of parallel lines 1 and 2, that are both intersected by a third line, such as line 3 in the diagram below, angle *A* and angle *D* are called alternate interior angles. Alternate interior angles have the same degree measurement. Angle *B* and angle *C* are also alternate interior angles.

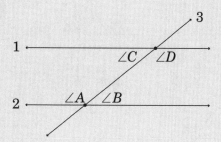

Alternate Exterior Angles

For any pair of parallel lines 1 and 2, that are both intersected by a third line, such as line 3 in the diagram below, angle *A* and angle *D* are called alternate exterior angles. Alternate exterior angles have the same degree measurement. Angle *B* and angle *C* are also alternate exterior angles.

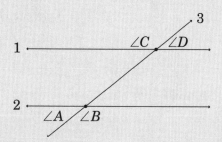

Corresponding Angles

For any pair of parallel lines 1 and 2, that are both intersected by a third line, such as line 3 in the diagram below, angle *A* and angle *C* are called corresponding angles. Corresponding angles have the same degree of measurement. Angle *B* and angle *D* are also corresponding angles.

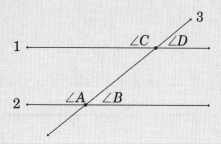

Angle Bisector

An angle bisector is a ray that divides an angle into two equal angles. The gray ray on the right is the angle bisector of the angle on the left.

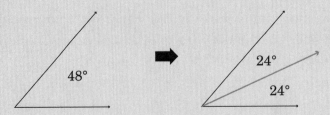

The gray ray on the right is the angle bisector of the angle on the left.

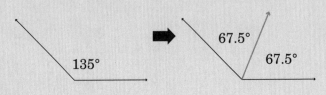

5.5: Vertical Angles

Definition: Two opposite angles formed by two intersecting lines; they are congruent (i.e., their measures are equal).

Example:

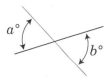

See Problems 53, 69, 71, and 94 for sample problems.

5.6: Supplementary Angles

Definition: Angles whose measures have a sum of 180°

Examples:

Example #1:

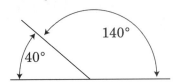

Example #2:

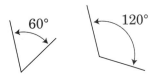

Problem 53

The measure of one of the angles in the figure below is 135°. Calculate the measures of the remaining angles.

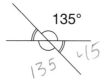

135°

135   45

Solution 53

If the measure of one angle is 135°, the opposite one will have the same measure by virtue of being vertical angles. The measure of the adjacent angle will be 180° − 135° = 45°, as they are supplementary angles. As a result, the measures of the four angles will be

$$45°, 135°, 45°, 135°$$

Problem 54

Calculate the measures of the angles a and b in the figure below.

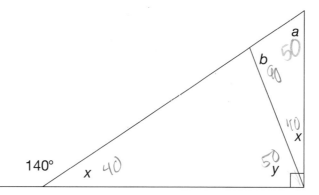

140°

Solution 54

Given that x and y are complementary and x and 140° are supplementary,
$$x + 140° = 180° \rightarrow x = 40°$$
$$x + y = 90° \rightarrow y = 90° - x = 50°$$
$$140° = \text{exterior angle} = 90° + a \rightarrow a = 50°$$
$$b + x + a = 180° \rightarrow b = 180° - 40° - 50° = 90°$$

Note: b doesn't appear to be a right angle but it turns out it is. This is an example reinforcing the rule that in geometry, unless specified in the problem or clearly indicated in the figure, you should treat every diagram as not drawn to scale.

5.7: Complementary Angles

Definition: Two angles whose measures add up to 90°.
Examples:

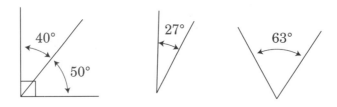

See Problem 54 for a sample problem.

5.8: Straight Angles

Definition: A straight angle is the angle formed by a straight line; its measure is 180°.
Example:

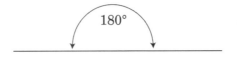

Problem 55

Calculate angle *b*.

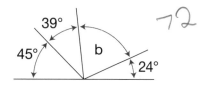

Solution 55

In this diagram angle *b* is simply 180°. Then, take away the sum of the other angles.

Sum of known angles = 45° + 39° + 24° = 108°

The measure of Angle *b* = 180° − 108° = 72°

5.9: Right Angles

Definition: A right angle is an angle with a measure of 90°.
Example:

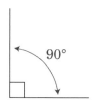

Problem 56

Given a right angle, what is the measure of its supplementary angle?

Solution 56

$$180° - 90° = 90°$$

The supplementary of a right angle is also a right angle.

5.10: Exterior Angles

Definition: An exterior angle is an angle formed by one side of a triangle and the extension of another side; its measure is equal to the sum of the measures of the two opposite interior angles (because they have the same supplementary angle; in the example below, 30°).

Example:

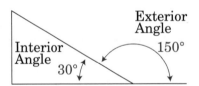

Problem 57

In $\triangle DEF$, an exterior angle at F is represented by $8x + 15$. If the two non-adjacent interior angles are represented by $4x + 5$ and $3x + 20$, find the value of x.

$$F \quad 8x + 15$$
$$D \quad 3x + 20 \qquad 4x + 5 \quad E$$

$$360 = \left(4x + 5\right) + \left(180 - 8x + 15\right) + \left(3x + 20\right)$$
$$220 \left(-x\right)$$

Solution 57

$$8x + 15 = (4x + 5) + (3x + 20)$$
$$8x + 15 = 7x + 25$$
$$8x = 7x + 10$$
$$x = 10$$

5.11: Polygon

Definition: A closed geometric figure made up of line segments.

Examples:

Convex: Concave:

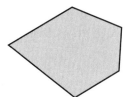

Problem 58

Calculate the sum of the interior angle measures of the polygon shown below.

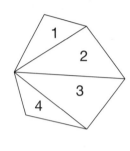

720

Solution 58

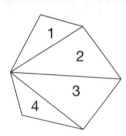

Subdivide the polygon into triangles. The number of triangles obtained is 4. The required measure is

$$4 \times 180° = 720°$$

Note: A formula can be easily derived based on the observation that there is only one parameter that describes the above figure (i.e., n = number of sides/internal angles/vertices). Based on the solution obtained above ($n = 6$), by extrapolation, the formula that gives the measure of the sum of interior angles in a polygon of n sides is:

$$(n-2) \times 180°$$

5.12: Diagonal

Definition: Line segment inside a polygon drawn from one vertex to another.

Example: A diagonal is a line segment connecting nonadjacent vertices of a polygon.

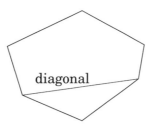

diagonal

Problem 59

Calculate the number of diagonals in an *n*-gon (a polygon with *n* sides).

Solution 59

Let us begin by drawing all diagonals from one vertex of the polygon. In the example above and in Problem 58, the number of diagonals is 3. If we consider a quadrilateral (a polygon with 4 sides), from one vertex we can draw only one diagonal. In a pentagon, we would be able to draw two diagonals. Analyzing these examples and extrapolating to polygons with "*n*" sides leads us to the conclusion that the number of diagonals that can be drawn from one vertex in an *n*-gon is equal to the number of sides (*n*) minus 3.

To calculate the total number of diagonals in an *n*-gon we now need to multiply the number of diagonals drawn from a vertex with the total number of vertices and divide by 2 to avoid counting diagonals connecting two vertices twice.

As a result, the formula for the total (maximum) number of diagonals in an *n*-gon is

$$\frac{n(n-3)}{2}$$

5.13: Triangle

Definition: A triangle is a polygon with three sides.

Example:

Perimeter: $p = a + b + c$

Area: $A = \dfrac{bh}{2}$ or $A = \dfrac{1}{2}bh$

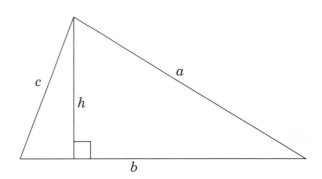

Problem 60

Two sides of a triangle are 4 and 13. If the third side is an integer, find the largest possible value for the perimeter of this triangle.

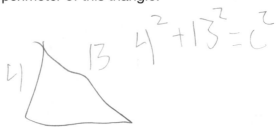

Solution 60

Let the third side be *x*. It follows (see Problem 20) that

$$13 - 4 < x < 13 + 4$$
$$9 < x < 17$$

The largest possible value of the perimeter of this triangle is obtained by considering the largest (integer) value for *x*, or 16. As a result, the answer is:

$$4 + 13 + 16 = 33$$

5.14: Acute Triangle

Definition: A triangle in which angles are all acute.
Example:

See Problem 62 for a sample problem.

5.15: Obtuse Triangle

Definition: A triangle with one obtuse and two acute angles.
Example:

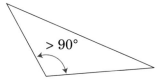

See Problem 67 for a sample problem.

5.16: Right Triangle

Definition: A triangle with a right angle and two obtuse (and complementary) ones.
Example:

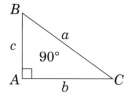

Pythagorean Theorem: $a^2 = b^2 + c^2$

The 30/60/90 triangle rule: Measure of Angle $C = 30°$, then $a = 2c$

See Problems 61 and 65 for sample problems.

5.17: Equilateral Triangle

Definition: Triangle characterized by having three equal sides and angles (each therefore measuring 60°).
Example:

See Problem 63 for a sample problem.

5.18: Isosceles Triangle

Definition: Triangles having two sides of equal length; the angles opposite the equal sides are also equal.
Example:

See Problems 64 and 65 for sample problems.

Problem 61

The right triangle shown below has an area of 25. Find its hypotenuse.

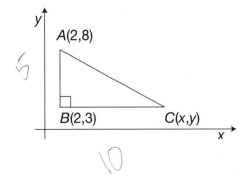

Solution 61

Because the *x* coordinates of points *A* and *B* are equal, segment *AB* is parallel to the *y* axis. Because *BC* is perpendicular to *AB*, then *BC* is parallel to the *x* axis and therefore the *y* coordinate of point *C* is equal to 3. We now need to find the *x* coordinate of point *C* using the area as follows (*d* = distance):

$$\text{area} = 25 = (\tfrac{1}{2})\, d(A, B) \times d(B, C)$$
$$d(A, B) = 8 - 3 = 5$$
$$d(B, C) = |x - 2|$$

We now substitute *d*(*A*, *B*) and *d*(*B*, *C*) in the area formula above to obtain

$$25 = (\tfrac{1}{2})\,(5)\,|x - 2|$$

We solve the above as follows

$$|x - 2| = 10$$
$$x = 12 \text{ and } x = -8$$

We select *x* = 12 because point *C* is to the right of point *B* and therefore its *x* coordinate is greater than 2.

We now have the coordinates of points *A* and *C* and we can next find the hypotenuse using the distance formula.

$$\text{Hypotenuse} = d(A, C) = \sqrt{(12 - 2)^2 + (3 - 8)^2}$$

$$= \sqrt{125} = 5\sqrt{5}$$

Problem 62

Triangle *ABC* shown below is inscribed inside a square of side 20 cm. Find the area of the triangle

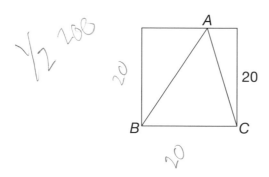

Solution 62

By definition, the area of the triangle = $\dfrac{base \times height}{2} = \dfrac{20 \times 20}{2} =$

200 cm²

Problem 63

Find the area of an equilateral triangle that has sides equal to 10 cm.

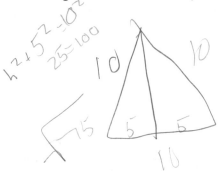

Solution 63

Let A, B, and C be the vertices of the equilateral triangle and M the mid-point of segment BC. Because the triangle is equilateral, $\triangle AMC$ is a right triangle. Let us find h, the height of $\triangle ABC$ using the Pythagorean theorem.

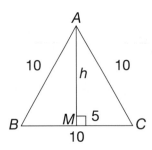

$$h^2 + 5^2 = 10^2$$

Solving the above equation for h leads to:
$$h = 5\sqrt{3} \ \text{cm}$$

We now find the area using the formula:

$$\text{area} = \frac{1}{2} \times \text{base} \times \text{height} = \frac{1}{2} \times 10 \times 5\sqrt{3} =$$

$$25\sqrt{3} \text{ cm}^2$$

Problem 64

In an isosceles triangle, the measure of angle A is 30 degrees greater than that of angle B. Calculate the largest value of the measure of angle C.

Solution 64

An isosceles triangle has two angles equal in size. The relationship between the measures of the angles A and B is summarized as follows:

$$A = B + 30°$$

Option #1: $C = A > B$

Let's now calculate the measures of all angles.

$$C = A = B + 30°$$
$$A + B + C = B + 30° + B + B + 30° = 180°$$
$$3 \times B = 120° \text{ or } B = 40°$$

Thus

$$A = 70° \; ; B = 40°; C = 70°$$

Option #2: $A > B = C$

$$A = B + 30°$$
$$B = C$$
$$A + B + C = B + 30° + B + B = 180°$$
$$3 \times B = 150° \text{ or } B = 50°$$

Thus

$$A = 80° \; ; B = 50°; C = 50°$$

Problem 65

What kind of triangles are obtained by dividing the area of a square with a diagonal? What are the measures of their angles?

Solution 65

The two triangles obtained are "right isosceles." The measure of the two equal angles is:

$$\frac{180° - 90°}{2} = 45°$$

On Your Own Problem 14

In isosceles triangle $\triangle ABC$, side $\overline{BC}$ is longer than the other two sides. If the degree measure of $\angle A$ is a multiple of 12, calculate the greatest possible measure of $\angle C$.

5.19: Hypotenuse

Definition: The longest side of a right triangle (opposite to the right angle); the other sides are called "legs."

Example:

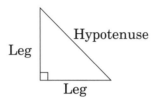

Problem 66

Compare the areas of the triangle (*A1*) and rectangle (*A2*) shown below. Indicate which area is the largest.

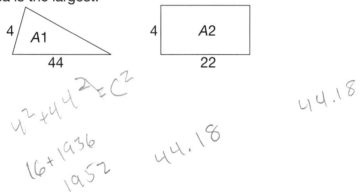

Solution 66

It makes sense to start with the formula that gives us the area of the triangle (*A1*):

$$A1 = \frac{base \times height}{2}$$

Redrawing the triangle helps:

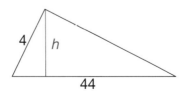

Rewriting the equation above leads to

$$A1 = \frac{44 \times h}{2} = 22 \times h$$

One should notice that comparing "$22 \times h$" and "88" is equivalent to comparing "h" and "4". As a result, it's easy to observe that we are now comparing a side (h) and the hypotenuse (4) of the triangle on the left. Given that the hypotenuse is longer than any sides,

$$h < 4$$

one concludes that the area of the triangle is less than 88 (see also Problem 1) or

$$A1 < 88 = 4 \times 22 = A2$$

And thus the answer is $A2$.

5.20: Congruent Triangles

Definition: Triangles that have the same size and shape.

Examples: Any one of the following four rules can be used to prove that two triangles are congruent:

- *Side-Angle-Side* (SAS) states that if two sides and the included angle are congruent to two sides and the included angle of a second triangle, the two triangles are congruent. An included angle is an angle created by two sides of a triangle.
- *Side-Side-Side* (SSS) states that if three sides of one triangle are congruent to three sides of a second triangle, the two triangles are congruent.
- *Angle-Side-Angle* (ASA) states that if two angles and the included side of one triangle are congruent to two angles and the included side of another triangle, the triangles are congruent. An included side is a side that is common to (between) two angles. For example, in the figure used in Problem 69, segments *AP* and *PD* are included sides between a 90° angle and angles *BPA* and *CPD*, respectively.
- *Angle-Angle-Side* (AAS) states that if two angles and a nonincluded side of one triangle are congruent to two angles and the corresponding nonincluded side of another triangle, the two triangles are congruent.

Note that when two triangles are congruent, all six pairs of corresponding parts (angles and sides) are congruent. This statement is referred to as the CPCTC rule (corresponding parts of congruent triangles are congruent).

Problem 67

Is triangle $\triangle PQR$ congruent to triangle $\triangle STV$ by SAS? Explain.

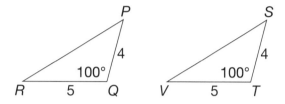

Solution 67

Segment PQ is congruent to segment ST because $PQ = ST = 4$.
Angle Q is congruent to angle T because angle Q = angle T = 100 degrees.
Segment QR is congruent to segment TV because $QR = TV = 5$.
Thus, triangle $\triangle PQR$ is congruent to triangle $\triangle STV$ by Side-Angle-Side.

Problem 68

Show that triangle $\triangle QYN$ is congruent to triangle $\triangle QYP$.

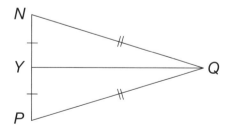

Solution 68

Segment *QN* is congruent to segment *QP* and segment *YN* is congruent to segment *YP* because that information is given in the figure.

Segment *YQ* is congruent to segment *YQ* by the Reflexive Property of Congruence, which says any figure is congruent to itself.

Thus, triangle △*QYN* is congruent to triangle △*QYP* by Side-Side-Side.

Problem 69

Show that triangle △*BAP* is congruent to triangle △*CDP*.

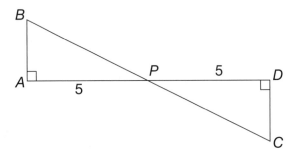

Solution 69

Angle *A* is congruent to angle *D* because they are both right angles.

Segment *AP* is congruent to segment *DP* because both have measures of 5.

Angle *BPA* and angle *CPD* are congruent because vertical angles are congruent.

Thus, triangle △*BAP* is congruent to triangle △*CDP* by Angle-Side-Angle.

Problem 70

Show that triangle $\triangle CAB$ is congruent to triangle $\triangle ZYX$.

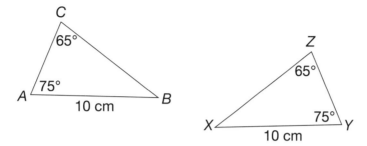

Solution 70

Angle A and angle Y are congruent because that information is given in the figure.

Angle C is congruent to angle Z because that information is given in the figure.

Segment AB corresponds to segment XY and they are congruent because that information is given in the figure.

Thus, triangle $\triangle CAB$ is congruent to triangle $\triangle ZYX$ by Angle-Angle-Side.

Problem 71

Prove that segment *BC* is congruent to segment *CE*.

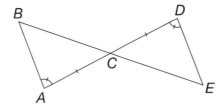

Solution 71

First, you have to prove that triangle △*CAB* is congruent to triangle △*CDE*.

Angle *A* is congruent to angle *D* because that information is given in the figure.

Segment *AC* is congruent to segment *CD* because that information is given in the figure.

Angle *BCA* is congruent to angle *DCE* because vertical angles are congruent.

Triangle △*CAB* is congruent to triangle △*CDE* by Angle-Side-Angle.

Now that we know the triangles are congruent, we also know that all corresponding parts must be congruent. Therefore, segment *BC* is congruent to segment *CE* by CPCTC.

5.21: Similar Triangles

Definition: Triangles that have the same shape, with each corresponding pair of angles having the same measure.

Example:

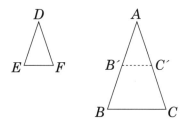

Problem 72

Which of the following sets of numbers could represent the sides of the triangle $\triangle ABC$ shown below?

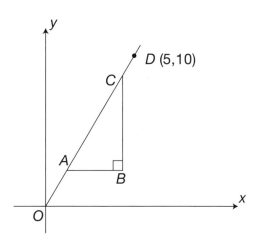

(A) $5, 10, \sqrt{125}$

(B) $2, 5, \sqrt{29}$

(C) $3, 6, \sqrt{45}$

(D) $3, 5, 6$

Solution 72

The triangle $\triangle ABC$ is a right triangle, so
$$AC^2 = AB^2 + BC^2 \text{ (Pythagorean Theorem)}$$

As a result, we can eliminate the answer that does not satisfy the above equation (D). In addition, A has to be ruled out because
$$AB < 5 \text{ and } BC < 10$$

To pick the correct answer between B and C, one notices that by drawing a perpendicular from point D to Ox, one obtains two similar triangles, $\triangle ABC$ and $\triangle OED$.

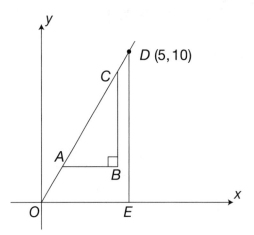

As a result,
$$\frac{AB}{BC} = \frac{OE}{ED} = \frac{5}{10} = \frac{1}{2}$$

Because the ratio of the two sides of triangle $\triangle ABC$ must be 1:2, the correct answer is C.

5.22: Altitude

Definition: Altitude (height) is perpendicular from a vertex to the opposite side of the triangle.

Example:

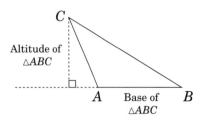

Problem 73

In the figure below, *AB* is parallel with *CD*, *BC* is parallel with *DA*, and *AB* = *BC*. Calculate the perimeter of *ABCD*.

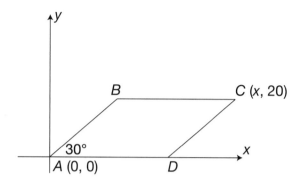

Solution 73

AB being parallel with *CD* and *BC* with *DA* results in *AB* = *CD* and *BC* = *DA*, so *ABCD* is a parallelogram. Given that two adjacent sides are equal (*AB* = *BC*), all sides are equal:

$$AB = BC = CD = DA$$

and thus the perimeter of *ABCD* = 4 × *AB*.

From the figure below

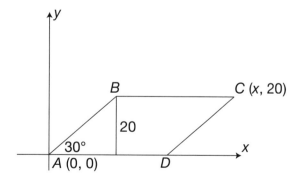

AB = 2 × 20 = 40 (the site opposing a 30° angle in a right triangle is half the hypotenuse). As a consequence, the perimeter of *ABCD* = 4 × 40 = 160.

5.23: Quadrilaterals

Definition: Quadrilaterals are two-dimensional geometric figures (polygons) with 4 sides and 2 diagonals, with 4 interior angles with a sum equaling 360 degrees.

Examples:

Special Quadrilaterals

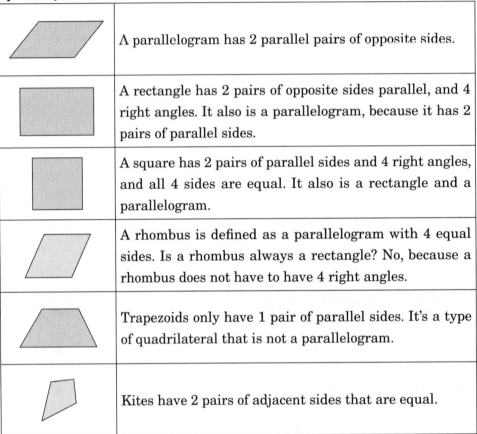

	A parallelogram has 2 parallel pairs of opposite sides.
	A rectangle has 2 pairs of opposite sides parallel, and 4 right angles. It also is a parallelogram, because it has 2 pairs of parallel sides.
	A square has 2 pairs of parallel sides and 4 right angles, and all 4 sides are equal. It also is a rectangle and a parallelogram.
	A rhombus is defined as a parallelogram with 4 equal sides. Is a rhombus always a rectangle? No, because a rhombus does not have to have 4 right angles.
	Trapezoids only have 1 pair of parallel sides. It's a type of quadrilateral that is not a parallelogram.
	Kites have 2 pairs of adjacent sides that are equal.

We can use a Venn diagram to group the types of quadrilaterals.

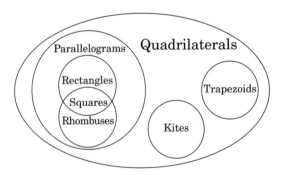

From this diagram, one can see that a square is a quadrilateral, a parallelogram, a rectangle, and a rhombus!

Is a rectangle always a rhombus? No, because all four sides of a rectangle don't have to be equal. However, the sets of rectangles and rhombuses do intersect, and their intersection is the set of squares—all squares are both a rectangle and a rhombus.

Is a trapezoid a parallelogram? No, because a trapezoid has only one pair of parallel sides. That is why we must show the set of trapezoids in a separate circle on the Venn diagram.

What about kites? Kites are quadrilaterals that can be parallelograms. If their two pairs of sides are equal, they become a rhombus, and if their angles are equal, they become a square.

Problem 74

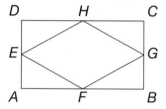

E, F, G, and H are the midpoints of the sides of rectangle ABCD. AB and BC are equal to 12 and 16, respectively. Calculate the difference between the area and the perimeter of quadrilateral EFGH.

Solution 74

Each side of the quadrilateral EFGH is the hypotenuse of a right triangle whose sides are equal to half the lengths of the sides of the rectangular ABCD (i.e., 6 and 8). As a result,

$$EF = FG = GH = HE = 6^2 + 8^2 = 36 + 64 = 100 = \sqrt{100} = 10$$

(The quadrilateral EFGH is therefore a rhombus.)

The perimeter of $EFGH = 4 \times 10 = 40$

Note that the corner triangles are equal (using the *side-angle-side* rule, i.e., right triangles having equal sides) and the area of each one is:

$$\frac{6 \times 8}{2} = 24$$

Area of $EFGH$ = Area of $ABCD - 4 \times$ Area of a corner triangle

The area of $EFGH = 12 \times 16 - 4 \times 24 = 192 - 96 = 96$

The difference between the area and the perimeter of $EFGH$ is therefore $96 - 40 = 56$.

5.24: Parallelograms

Definition: Quadrilateral with opposite angles of equal measure and opposite sides of equal length.

Example:

Perimeter: $p = b + b + c + c$ Area: $A = bh$
or $p = 2b + 2c$

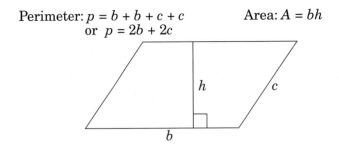

See Problem 73 for a sample problem.

5.25: Rectangles

Definition: Parallelogram in which all angles are right angles.

Example:

Perimeter: $p = 2(l + w)$ Area: $A = lw$
or $p = 2l + 2w$

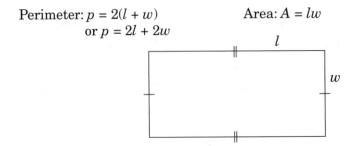

See Problems 76, 142, and 160 for sample problems.

5.26: Squares

Definition: Rectangle in which the length of all sides are equal (it is sufficient to say that it is a parallelogram with equal adjacent sides).
Example:

Area = L^2 where L is the side length

See Problems 76, 116, and 142 for sample problems.

Problem 75

The diagonals of *ABCD* (see below), *AC* = 30 and *BD* = 40, are perpendicular to each other and *AB* = 15. Calculate the area of *ABCD*.

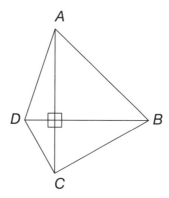

Solution 75

Solution #1

Observe that the area of *ABCD* is actually half the area of the rectangle shown below:

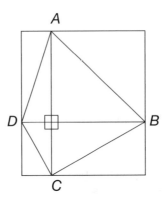

therefore the area of $ABCD = \dfrac{(AC \times BD)}{2} = \dfrac{(30 \times 40)}{2} = 600$

Solution #2

Using notations shown in the figure below (see also Problem 5),

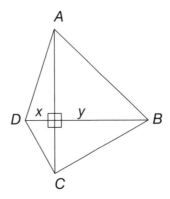

Area of $ABCD$ = Area of $\triangle ACD$ + Area of $\triangle ABC$ =

$$= \frac{x \times AC}{2} + \frac{y \times AC}{2} =$$

$$= \frac{AC}{2}(x + y) = \frac{AC \times BD}{2} =$$

$$= \frac{30 \times 40}{2} = 600$$

5.27: Perimeter

Definition: The perimeter (of a polygon) is the sum of the lengths of its sides.

Example: For a square with side length $= L$, the perimeter $= 4L$.

Problem 76

The areas of two squares with sides representing the length and the width of a rectangle are 100 and 64 inches, respectively. Calculate the perimeter of the rectangle.

Solution 76

Given a rectangle with length $= L$ and width $= W$, its perimeter (P) is $2 \times (L + W)$. With these notations, we can write the following equations:

$$L = \sqrt{100} = 10$$

$$W = \sqrt{64} = 8$$

$$P = 2 \times (L + W) = 36$$

5.28: Regular Polygon

Definition: A regular (or equilateral) polygon is one with sides that all have the same length and angles that all have the same measure.

Example: A polygon with 5 equal sides:

Problem 77

Calculate the angles of a regular polygon with 8 sides.

Solution 77

The internal angles of a regular polygon are equal. The sum of the measures of the internal angles is

$$(n-2) \times 180° = 6 \times 180° = 1080° \text{ (see also Problem 58)}$$

The measure of each angle is

$$\frac{1080°}{8} = 135°$$

5.29: Circle

Definition: The two-dimensional geometric figure that includes all of the points that are at the same distance from one fixed point called the center.

Example:

Perimeter: $C = \pi d$ or $C = 2\pi r$
(Circumference)

Area: $A = \pi r^2$

Note: The value of π is 3.1415926 (to 7 decimal places)

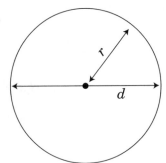

Problem 78

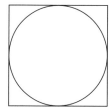

The figure above shows a circle inscribed in a square (i.e., the sides of the square are tangent to the circle).

If the radius of the circle (r) is 8 and the length of each side of the square (L) is π, calculate the ratio of

1. the circumferences of the circle and the square
2. the areas of the circle and the square

Solution 78

The circle:

$$\text{Circumference} = 2\pi r$$
$$\text{Area} = \pi r^2$$

The square:

$$\text{Circumference} = 4\pi$$
$$\text{Area} = \pi^2$$

The required ratios are:

$$\text{ratio of circumferences} = \frac{16\pi}{4\pi} = 4$$

$$\text{ratio of areas} = \frac{64\pi}{\pi^2} = \frac{64}{\pi}$$

On Your Own Problem 15

Consider two circles, one having a radius that is five times the radius of the other. What is the greatest possible number of points of intersection of the two circles?

On Your Own Problem 16

In the coordinate plane, calculate the coordinates of the center of a circle knowing that the points $A(4,1)$, $B(-2,1)$ and $C(1,4)$ lie on the circle.

5.30: Diameter

Definition: The diameter (of a circle) is a line segment that passes through the center and has its endpoints on the circle; it's the longest line segment that can be drawn in a circle.

Example:

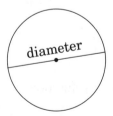

See Problem 79 for a sample problem.

5.31: Radius

Definition: The radius (of a circle) is a line segment extending from the center to a point on the circle).

Example:

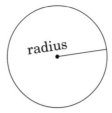

Problem 79

The area of a circle is 314 cm². Calculate an approximate value for its diameter.

Solution 79

Let the diameter of the circle be *d*.

$$A = \pi \times r^2 = 314$$

$$\pi = 3.141... \simeq 3.14$$

$$d = 2 \times r = 2 \times \sqrt{\frac{314}{\pi}} \simeq$$

$$\simeq 2 \times \sqrt{100} = 20 \ [cm]$$

5.32: Arc

Definition: The arc of a circle is a part of a circle measured in degrees or units of length; it consists of two points of the circle and all of the points between them.

Example: An arc is a part of the circumference/edge of a circle.

Arc = connected section of the circumference of a circle.

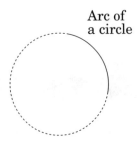

Arc of
a circle

Arcs are measured in two ways: as the measure of the central angle, or as the length of the arc itself.

Measurement by central angle (degrees):

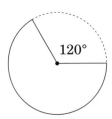

120°

The dotted arc (minor arc) measures 120°.

The black arc (major arc) measures 240°.

Measurement by arc length (radians):

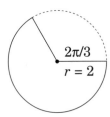

2π/3
$r = 2$

Formula: $s = r\theta$

s = arc length

r = radius of the circle

θ = measure of the central angle in radians

Gray arc: $r = 2$ and $\theta = 2\pi/3$, so $s = 4\pi/3$

Black arc: $r = 2$ and $\theta = 4\pi/3$, so $s = 8\pi/3$

5.33: Tangent Line

Definition: A tangent is a line that touches a curve at a point without crossing over. Formally, it is a line that intersects a curve at a point where the slope of the curve equals the slope of the line.

Example:

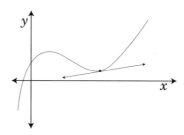

See Problem 80 for a sample problem.

5.34: Tangent to a Circle

Definition: A line that intersects a circle at exactly one point; it's always perpendicular to the radius that contains the one point of the line that touches the circle (i.e., to the point of tangency).

Example:

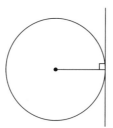

Problem 80

A line (n) is tangent to a circle in A(5,1). The circle's center is O(4,2). Calculate the slope of line (n).

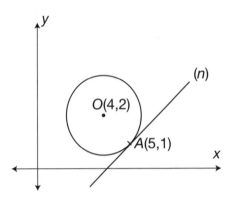

Solution 80

Because line (n) is tangent to the circle in A, the line passes through O (the center of the circle) and A is perpendicular to line (n). If two lines are perpendicular to each other, the product of their slopes (see Section 4.14) is equal to –1, so

$$\text{Slope of } (n) \times \text{slope of } OA = -1$$

Solution #1:

$$\text{Slope of } OA = \frac{\Delta y}{\Delta x} = \frac{2-1}{4-5} = -1$$

$$\text{Slope of } (n) = \frac{-1}{-1} = 1$$

Solution #2 (for students who tend to overanalyze, but this is an overkill):

Using the general equation of a line (y = mx + b) twice for OA—as (4, 2) and (5, 1) both belong to line segment OA—leads to:

$$2 = 4m + b$$
$$1 = 5m + b$$

If one subtracts the first equation from the second, the result is

$$-1 = m$$

Thus, the slope of (n)

$$= \frac{-1}{m} = \frac{-1}{-1} = 1$$

5.35: Circumference

Definition: The circumference of a circle is the distance/length around the circle (perimeter).

Example: Circumference also means a complete circular arc (the distance around the outside of a circle).

Circumference: $C = \pi d$
  or $C = 2\pi r$
  (d = diameter)

Area: $A = \pi r^2$

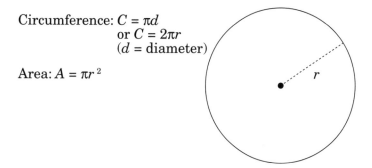

See Problems 81 and 175 for sample problems.

5.36: Central Angle

Definition: A central angle is an angle that has its vertex at the center of the circle.

Example:

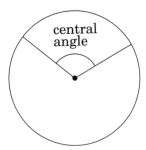

See Problems 81 and 175 for sample problems.

5.37: Area of a Sector and Arc Length

Definition: See illustration under example below.

Example:

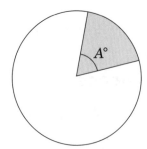

The shaded area is called a sector. The part of the circumference of the circle that is on the edge of the sector is called an arc.

Let us denote the measure of the central angle ($A°$), the area of the sector, and the arc length by MCA, AS, and AL, respectively.

MCA	Sector Area	Arc Length
360°	πr^2	$2\pi r$
$A°$	AS	AL

Given that the above quantities are directly proportional, the formulas for AS and AL corresponding to a central angle with a measure of A° is:

$$\frac{360°}{A°} = \frac{\pi r^2}{AS} \qquad AS = \frac{\pi r^2 \times A°}{360°}$$

$$\frac{360°}{A°} = \frac{2\pi r}{AL} \qquad AL = \frac{2\pi r \times A°}{360°} = \frac{\pi r \times A°}{180°}$$

5.38: Solid Geometry

The following table summarizes useful solid geometry formulas.

	Rectangular Solid	Cylinder	Cone	Pyramid	Sphere
Volume	lwh	$\pi r^2 h$	$\dfrac{\pi r^2 h}{3}$	$\dfrac{Bh}{3}$ (B = base area)	$\dfrac{4\pi r^3}{3}$
Surface Area	$2(lw + wh + lh)$	$2\pi r^2 + 2\pi rh$	$\pi r^2 + \pi rl$	B + areas of four triangular faces	$4\pi r^2$

Problem 81

One slice is cut and removed from a cake of circular shape with area equal to 100π cm^2. Assuming the top view of it corresponds to the gray sector shown in the diagram on p. 144, and considering the problem as being two-dimensional (i.e., the thickness of the cake is negligible compared to the radius), calculate with approximation (1) the perimeter (circumference) and (2) area of the leftover piece assuming the measure of the central angle A to be 30°.

Solution 81

The radius of the circle is

$$r = \sqrt{\frac{A}{\pi}} = \sqrt{\frac{100\pi}{\pi}} = \sqrt{100} = 10$$

The arc length corresponding to a central angle of 30° is

$$2\pi r \times \frac{30}{360} = 2\pi r \times \frac{1}{12}$$

1. The perimeter/circumference of the "remaining" cake is

$$\left(2\pi r - 2\pi r \times \frac{1}{12}\right) + 2r = 2\pi r \times \frac{11}{12} + 2r =$$

$$2 \times 10 \times \left(\pi + \frac{11}{12}\right) \approx 20 \times 4 = 80$$

The area of the arc sector corresponding to the "slice" is

$$\pi r^2 \times \frac{30}{360} = \frac{\pi r^2}{12}$$

2. The area of the "remaining" cake is

$$\pi r^2 - \frac{\pi r^2}{12} = \frac{11 \times \pi r^2}{12} = \frac{\pi \times 1100}{12} \approx 288$$

On Your Own Problem 17

Calculate the volume of a rectangular solid (in cubic inches) if eight of its edges each have a length of 4 inches and the other four each have a length of 8 inches.

Chapter

Trigonometry

The greatest enemy of knowledge is not ignorance;
it's the illusion of knowledge.

—Stephen Hawking

6.1: Right Triangle

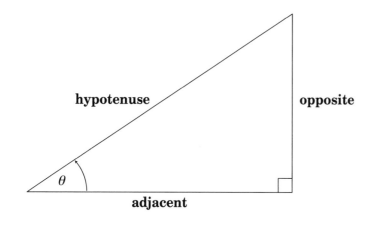

$$\sin \theta = \frac{\text{opp}}{\text{hyp}} \qquad \csc \theta = \frac{\text{hyp}}{\text{opp}}$$

$$\cos \theta = \frac{\text{adj}}{\text{hyp}} \qquad \sec \theta = \frac{\text{hyp}}{\text{adj}}$$

$$\tan \theta = \frac{\text{opp}}{\text{adj}} \qquad \cot \theta = \frac{\text{adj}}{\text{opp}}$$

6.2: Unit Circle

Definitions:

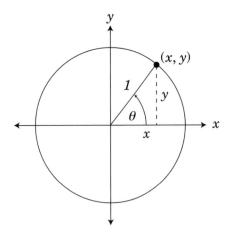

$$\sin\theta = \frac{y}{1} \qquad \csc\theta = \frac{1}{y}$$

$$\cos\theta = \frac{x}{1} \qquad \sec\theta = \frac{1}{x}$$

$$\tan\theta = \frac{y}{x} \qquad \cot\theta = \frac{x}{y}$$

6.3: Degrees to Radians Conversion

Definitions:

$$\frac{\pi}{180°} = \frac{t}{x} \quad\Rightarrow\quad t = \frac{\pi x}{180°} \quad\text{and}\quad x = \frac{180° t}{\pi}$$

where x and t are angles in degrees and radians, respectively.

6.4: Trigonometric Functions

Domains:

$\sin\theta, \quad \forall\theta \in (-\infty, \infty)$

$\csc\theta, \quad \forall\theta \neq n\pi, \text{ where } n \in Z$

$\cos\theta, \quad \forall\theta \in (-\infty, \infty)$

$\sec\theta, \quad \forall\theta \neq \left(n + \frac{1}{2}\right)\pi, \text{ where } n \in Z$

$\tan\theta, \quad \forall\theta \neq \left(n + \frac{1}{2}\right)\pi, \text{ where } n \in Z$

$\cot\theta, \quad \forall\theta \neq n\pi, \text{ where } n \in Z$

Ranges:

$-1 \leq \sin\theta \leq 1$

$-1 \leq \cos\theta \leq 1$

$-\infty \leq \tan\theta \leq \infty$

$\csc\theta \geq 1 \text{ and } \csc\theta \leq -1$

$\sec\theta \geq 1 \text{ and } \sec\theta \leq -1$

$-\infty \leq \cot\theta \leq \infty$

Even/Odd Functions:

$$\sin(-\theta) = -\sin\theta \qquad \csc(-\theta) = -\csc\theta$$
$$\cos(-\theta) = \cos\theta \qquad \sec(-\theta) = \sec\theta$$
$$\tan(-\theta) = -\tan\theta \qquad \cot(-\theta) = -\cot\theta$$

Periodic Functions:

$$f(\theta + T) = f(\theta)$$

$$\sin(\theta + 2\pi n) = \sin\theta \qquad \csc(\theta + 2\pi n) = \csc\theta$$
$$\cos(\theta + 2\pi n) = \cos\theta \qquad \sec(\theta + 2\pi n) = \sec\theta$$
$$\tan(\theta + \pi n) = \tan\theta \qquad \cot(\theta + \pi n) = \cot\theta$$

where n = integer

6.5: Miscellaneous Identities

$$\tan\theta = \frac{\sin\theta}{\cos\theta} \qquad \cot\theta = \frac{\cos\theta}{\sin\theta}$$

$$\sin\theta = \frac{1}{\csc\theta} \qquad \csc\theta = \frac{1}{\sin\theta}$$

$$\cos\theta = \frac{1}{\sec\theta} \qquad \sec\theta = \frac{1}{\cos\theta}$$

$$\tan\theta = \frac{1}{\cot\theta} \qquad \cot\theta = \frac{1}{\tan\theta}$$

6.6: Pythagorean Identities

$$\sin^2\theta + \cos^2\theta = 1$$
$$\tan^2\theta + 1 = \sec^2\theta$$
$$1 + \cot^2\theta = \csc^2\theta$$

Problem 82

In a right triangle, the two angles that are not 90° measure $a°$ and $b°$. If $\sin a° = \dfrac{3}{5}$, calculate the value of the expression $\sin b° + \cos\left(90° - a°\right)$.

Solution 82

Let's use the figure below to illustrate the problem.

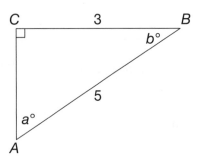

According to the Pythagorean Theorem, $AC^2 = 5^2 - 3^2 = 16$ or $AC = 4$. As a result,

$$\sin b° = \frac{AC}{AB} = \frac{4}{5}$$

Also, $\cos\left(90° - a°\right) = \sin a° = \dfrac{3}{5}$ and therefore

$$\sin b° + \cos\left(90° - a°\right) = \frac{4}{5} + \frac{3}{5} = \frac{7}{5}.$$

Problem 83

Let $x°$ and $y°$ be two acute angles and $\sin x° = \cos y°$. If $x = 2n - 11$ and $y - 4n - 7$, calculate n.

Solution 83

First, $\sin x° = \cos\left(90° - x°\right) = \cos y°$ or $y = 90 - x$.

Substituting the expressions in n for x and y, we obtain:
$4n - 7 = 90 - \left(2n - 11\right) = 101 - 2n$ or $6n = 108$. As a result,

$n = \dfrac{108}{6} = 16$

Problem 84

Triangles $\triangle ABC$ and $\triangle DEF$ are similar, with vertices D, E, F corresponding to vertices A, B, C, respectively. Given that

$$\angle ACB = 90°,\ AC = 6,\ AB = 10,\ \text{and}\ \frac{AB}{DE} = 5,$$

calculate the expression $\dfrac{AC}{DF}\cos x°$.

Solution 84

The figure below illustrates the problem we need to solve:

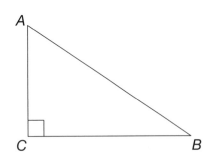 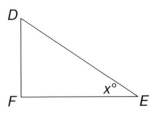

In the right triangle $\triangle ABC$, $CB^2 = AB^2 - AC^2 = 100 - 36 = 64$ or $CB = 8$. Also,

$$\cos x° = \frac{FE}{DE} = \frac{CB}{AB} = \frac{8}{10} = \frac{4}{5}$$

and

$$\frac{AC}{DF} = \frac{AB}{DE} = 5$$

As a result,

$$\frac{AC}{DF} \cos x° = 5 \times \frac{4}{5} = 4$$

Chapter 7

Miscellaneous Topics

Thunder is impressive, but it is lightning that does the work.

—Mark Twain

7.1: Average/Arithmetic Mean

Definition: The average/arithmetic mean of a list of values is the sum of the values divided by the number of values in the list.

Examples:

Example #1 (odd amount of numbers):

2, 4, 4, 5, 11, 28, 100

$$\text{Average} = \frac{(2+4+4+5+11+28+100)}{7} = 22$$

Example #2 (even amount of numbers):

2, 4, 4, 5, 11, 14, 28, 100

$$\text{Average} = \frac{(2+4+4+5+11+14+28+100)}{8} = 21$$

See Problems 85, 133, 151, 156, and 189 for sample problems.

On Your Own Problem 18

In a research center, the average (arithmetic mean) age of 25 scientists working on a government funded project is 40. After 5 more scientists are hired for the same project, the average age dropped to 39. Calculate the average age of the 5 newly hired scientists.

On Your Own Problem 19

Three years ago, the average (arithmetic mean) number of rare coins owned by 10 collectors was 85. Today, 3 collectors updated their numbers, as in the past 3 years, they acquired additional coins. The original numbers—60, 70, and 48—were replaced by 80, 90, and 108, respectively. Calculate the correct average number of rare coins owned by the 10 collectors today.

7.2: Median

Definition: The median is the middle value of a list of ordered numbers.

Examples: Based on the examples given for "average/arithmetic mean" (Section 7.1):

Example #1: 5

Example #2: $\frac{5+11}{2} = 8$

Note: When a list contains an even number of values, the median is the average of the two values positioned in the middle of the ordered list.

See Problems 85, 121, and 156 for sample problems.

On Your Own Problem 20

9, 1, 16, 6

The average (arithmetic mean) of five positive numbers is the same as the median of the same numbers. If four of the five numbers are shown above and the fifth is x, calculate all possible positive integer values for x.

7.3: Mode

Definition: Mode (of a list of values) is the value or values that appear the greatest number of times.

Examples: Based on the examples given for "average/arithmetic mean" (Section 7.1):

Example #1: 4

Example #2: 4

Problem 85

A number is added to the following list of numbers:
4, 6, 10, 10

Calculate the new addition to the list given that the average is equal to the median value of the list. In addition, calculate the mode of the complete list.

Solution 85

Let the new number be N. The average value of the sequence is

$$ave = \frac{N + 4 + 6 + 10 + 10}{5} = 6 + \frac{N}{5} > 6$$

If $N < 6$, the median is 6 and the condition that the average = median value is not satisfied.

Option #1: $6 < N < 10$; median = N, thus

$$6 + \frac{N}{5} = N \Rightarrow \frac{4N}{5} = 6 \Rightarrow N = 7.5$$

Option #2: $N > 10$; median = 10, thus

$$6 + \frac{N}{5} = 10 \Rightarrow \frac{N}{5} = 4 \Rightarrow N = 20$$

For both options, the mode of the sequence is 10.

7.4: Weighted Average

Definition: The weighted average is the average of two or more groups that do not all have the same number of members.

Example: Calculating the weighted average is devising a method of computing a kind of arithmetic mean of a set of numbers in which some elements of the set carry more importance (weight) than others.

Problem 86

Grades are often computed using a weighted average. Suppose that homework counts 10%, quizzes 20%, and tests 70%. Calculate Pat's overall grade if her average/total grades in homework, quizzes, and tests were 92, 68, and 81, respectively.

Solution 86

Pat's overall grade = $(0.10 \times 92) + (0.20 \times 68) + (0.70 \times 81) = 79.5$

7.5: Probability

Definition: The probability that an event will occur is a number between 0 and 1, inclusive. It's usually written as a fraction and indicates how likely it is that the event will happen. If the event is certain, its probability is 1. If an event is impossible, its probability is 0.

Example:

Let $P(A)$ be the probability of event A to occur:

$$P(A) = \frac{\text{number of outcomes of event } A}{\text{total number of outcomes in the sample size}}$$

Four basic rules of probabilities apply:

1. For any event A, $0 \leq P(A) \leq 1$.
2. P(impossible event) = 0. Also written P(empty set) = 0 or $P(\emptyset) = 0$.
3. P(sure event) = 1. Also written $P(S) = 1$, where S is the sample space.
4. P(not A) = 1 – $P(A)$ or P(complement of A) = 1 – $P(A)$ or $P(AC)$ = 1 – $P(A)$ or $P(\bar{A}) = 1 - P(A)$.

Problems 87 and 88

A jar contains only black and white marbles. If 1 marble is removed at random, the probability that it is black is $\frac{3}{5}$. After putting another 100 black marbles in the jar, the probability of drawing a black marble is $\frac{4}{5}$.

Problem 87: If one marble is initially removed at random, what is the probability that it is not black?

Problem 88: How many marbles were originally in the jar?

Solutions 87 and 88

Solution 87:
Because the probability that it is black is $\frac{3}{5}$, the probability of not being black is $1 - \frac{3}{5} = \frac{2}{5}$

Solution 88:
Let P_B be the probability of drawing a black marble. If the original number of black and white marbles were B and W, respectively, using the definition of probabilities one can write that

$$P_B = \frac{B}{B+W} = \frac{3}{5}$$

If 100 black marbles are added to the mix, the probability of drawing a black marble is

$$\frac{B+100}{B+100+W} = \frac{4}{5}$$

Let's now combine and solve the two equations above for B and W:

$$5B = 3B + 3W$$
$$5B + 500 = 4B + 4W + 400$$

or

$$2B = 3W$$
$$B = 4W - 100$$

If you multiply the second equation by 2 and substitute $3W$ for $2B$ from the first equation, you obtain

$$2B = 8W - 200 = 3W \text{ or } 5W = 200.$$

Consequently, $W = 40$ and $B = \frac{(3 \times 40)}{2} = 60$. The original number of black and white marbles in the jar was

$$B + W = 100$$

On Your Own Problem 21

In a jar, there are 45 red, 13 blue, and 33 green marbles. If one marble is to be chosen at random, calculate the probability that the chosen one is blue.

On Your Own Problem 22

If one of the positive factors of 60 is to be chosen at random, what is the probability that the chosen factor will not be a multiple of 5?

7.6: Independent Events

Definition: Events are independent if the outcome of either event has no effect on the other.

Examples: Independent events are those for which the probability of any one event occurring is unaffected by the occurrence or nonoccurrence of any of the other events. Two separate tosses of a fair coin are independent events. The result of the first toss has no effect on the probability of heads or tails on the second toss.

Problem 89

An opaque jar contains 5 red, 4 yellow, and 6 green candies. A child is allowed to pick two candies. What is the probability (1) of getting a green followed by a red candy and (2) of getting a red and then either a green or a yellow candy?

Solution 89

(1) $\dfrac{6}{5+4+6} \times \dfrac{5}{5+4+6-1} = \dfrac{6}{15} \times \dfrac{5}{14} = \dfrac{1}{7}$

(2) $\dfrac{5}{5+4+6} \times \dfrac{6}{5+4+6-1} +$

$\dfrac{5}{5+4+6} \times \dfrac{4}{5+4+6-1} =$

$= \dfrac{5}{15} \times \dfrac{6}{14} + \dfrac{5}{15} \times \dfrac{4}{14} =$

$\dfrac{1}{7} + \dfrac{2}{21} = \dfrac{5}{21}$

The probability of satisfying both conditions (i.e., 1 and 2) is therefore $\dfrac{1}{7} \times \dfrac{5}{21} = \dfrac{5}{147}$.

Note: "AND" = × (multiplication) and "OR" = + (addition)

Chapter 8

Problems by Degree of Difficulty and Type

Mathematics is the door and key to the sciences.

—Roger Bacon

SAT problems are currently assigned by the College Board three difficulty levels: *easy*, *medium*, and *hard*. Both math sections contained in an SAT test include *multiple-choice* and *open-ended* questions/problems.

To allow students to pick and choose problems by content, each problem in this chapter was assigned a qualifier to designate the main area of math in which knowledge is required in order to solve the problem, as well as whether the problem is a word problem or not. The latter qualifier was added to allow students not only to practice the factual knowledge in a particular field but also select problems that emphasize analytic/critical thinking skills. The qualifiers are: *arithmetic skills* (including numbers, operations, etc.), *algebra* (including functions), *geometry* (including measurements), *miscellaneous* (including data analysis, statistics, probability, etc.), and *word* (for word problems).

8.1: Easy Problems; Multiple Choice

Problem 90 (Word, Algebra)

The function shown below is used to predict the number of adults (A) accompanying their children to a water park:

$$A(T) = 2(120 - T)(T - 75)$$

where T° F is the expected high temperature for that day. The expected temperatures for Saturday and Sunday are 80° F and 85° F, respectively. Based on this model, calculate how many more adults are expected to come to the park on Sunday than on Saturday.

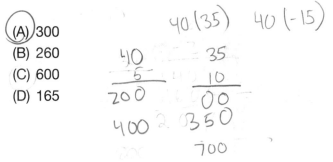

(A) 300

(B) 260

(C) 600

(D) 165

Problem 91 (Word, Algebra)

If x is 7 less than twice the product of y and z, calculate an expression for x in terms of y and z.

(A) $7 - 2yz$

(B) $2yz - 7$

(C) $7 - 2(y + z)$

(D) $2(y + z) - 7$

Problem 92 (Word, Algebra)

All 15 students in a music class completed the study of 4 required classic piano concerts. In addition, 3 of them completed the study of 5 contemporary piano compositions, and 5 students gave a recital during which they played a piano work by an American composer. Calculate the total number of assignments completed by the students in this music class.

(A) 20
(B) 23
(C) 33
(D) 80

$$15(4) = 60$$

Problem 93 (Word, Geometry)

Consider two circles, one having a radius that is 3 times the radius of the other. What is the greatest possible number of points of intersection of the two circles?

(A) 0
(B) 1
(C) 2
(D) 3

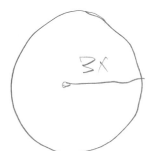

Problem 94 (Geometry)

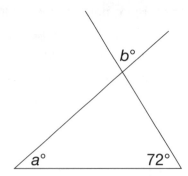

What is the measure of angle $b°$ shown in the figure above if $a° = 58°$?

(A) 60
(B) 78
(C) 52
(D) 50

Problem 95 (Word, Arithmetic Skills)

Assuming Michael runs at a constant pace and needs 15 minutes to complete a lap around his school's football field, calculate how much of a lap he will cover in 6 minutes.

(A) $\dfrac{4}{15}$

(B) $\dfrac{3}{5}$

(C) $\dfrac{15}{6}$

(D) $\dfrac{2}{5}$

Problem 96 (Word, Algebra)

Jessica needs to buy tomatoes. She finds that her neighborhood supermarket sells them in boxes that contain t tomatoes each. She ends up buying b boxes for which she pays d dollars. Assuming the tomatoes are equal in size and weight, which of the following formulas gives the price of a tomato?

(A) $\dfrac{d}{bt}$

(B) $\dfrac{b}{dt}$

(C) btd

(D) $\dfrac{dt}{b}$

$P =$

Problem 97 (Algebra)

Calculate the value of x^3y^2 if $x = y$ and $y = 2$.

(A) 8
(B) 32
(C) 16
(D) 24

8 4

Problem 98 (Arithmetic Skills)

Which of the following values could be equal to x if $\dfrac{2x}{7}$ is an integer?

(A) −14

(B) $\dfrac{7}{3}$

(C) −5

(D) 4

Problem 99 (Arithmetic Skills)

Calculate the number of positive integers less than 25 that are equal to 3 times an odd integer.

(A) 6

(B) 3

(C) 4

(D) 2

Problem 100 (Geometry)

The degree measures of three of the four angles of a quadrilateral are in the ratio of 2:3:5. The fourth angle measures 60°. Calculate the degree measure of the largest angle of the quadrilateral.

(A) 150°

(B) 240°

(C) 180°

(D) 90°

Problem 101 (Geometry)

The size of a rectangular closet is 1 ft x 2 ft. If the floor is to be covered with square tiles of side length equal to 4 in, how many tiles will be needed?

(A) 16
(B) 24
(C) 36
(D) 18

Problem 102 (Arithmetic Skills)

Calculate a possible value of an integer given that if divided by 2 and 3, the remainders are 0 and 1, respectively.

(A) 19
(B) 22
(C) 23
(D) 24

Problem 103 (Algebra)

If $\dfrac{8}{x} = y$ and $x = 2$, calculate the expression $x^2(y-1)$.

(A) 10
(B) 8
(C) 16
(D) 12

Problem 104 (Word, Arithmetic Skills)

There are 16 boys and 8 girls in a class. The day before Thanksgiving, all girls showed up at school, but the number of boys who were present represented 25% of the total student population. How many boys were absent that day?

(A) 16
(B) 18
(C) 20
(D) 10

Problem 105 (Algebra)

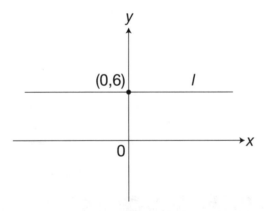

In the figure above, line *l* is perpendicular to the *y*-axis and intersects it 6 units away from the *x*-axis. Which one of the following points is on line *l*?

(A) (6, 1)
(B) (6, 0)
(C) (1, 0)
(D) (2, 6)

Problem 106 (Algebra)

If $3^{2x} = 729$, then $x =$

(A) 1
(B) 2
(C) 3
(D) 6

Problem 107 (Word, Arithmetic Skills)

When 250 pigeons raised and trained on a farm were released, only 50 did not reach the destination 50 miles away. What fraction of the pigeons that were released reached the destination?

(A) $\dfrac{4}{5}$

(B) $\dfrac{4}{9}$

(C) $\dfrac{6}{9}$

(D) $\dfrac{3}{5}$

Problem 108 (Word, Algebra)

A 56 centimeter-long piece of tape is 8 centimeters longer than 3 times the length of a shorter piece of tape. Calculate the length of the shorter piece of tape.

(A) 48
(B) 24
(C) 16
(D) 28

Problem 109 (Word, Algebra)

PRICES

	Bed	Table
1999	$240	$25
2004	$265	$30
2009	$280	$36

INVENTORY

	Warehouse		
	A	B	C
Beds	30	80	30
Tables	125	200	140

The table above gives the prices of the most popular styles of beds and tables manufactured by a furniture company in 3 different years. The second table gives the maximum number of beds and tables that can be stocked in each of the three warehouses (A, B, and C) owned by the manufacturer. Calculate the maximum possible value of the bed and table inventory in warehouse B in 1999.

(A) $21,600
(B) $24,400
(C) $22,200
(D) $24,200

Problem 110 (Word, Miscellaneous)

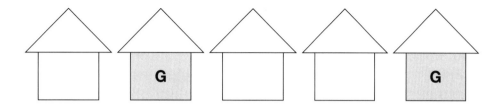

Eastside Blvd.

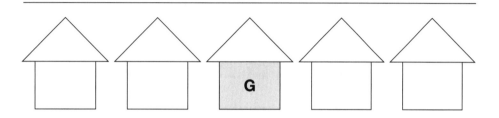

Five houses on each side of Eastside Blvd. are shown in the above figure. A town ordinance requires that no two houses directly across from each other on opposite sides of the street and no two houses next to each other on the same side of the street be painted the same color. If the houses labeled "G" in the figure above are painted gray, how many of the remaining houses can be painted gray?

(A) 6
(B) 4
(C) 1
(D) 5

Problem 111 (Algebra)

Calculate x if $2x - y = 7$ and $3x + 2y = 35$.

(A) 4
(B) 21
(C) 7
(D) 5

Problem 112 (Word, Miscellaneous)

Which of the following statements must be true given that Monica is older than John, who's older than Briana but younger than Luke?

(A) Luke is younger than Briana
(B) Luke is older than Monica
(C) Briana is younger than Luke
(D) Briana is older than Luke

Problem 113 (Algebra)

Calculate the value of $5a$ given that $3a - 2b = 4b$ and $2b = 3$.

(A) 15
(B) 8
(C) 25
(D) 10

Problem 114 (Word, Algebra)

Running at a constant rate, it takes Bobby 3 hours to finish a 15-mile race. George runs at a rate that is $\frac{1}{5}$ of Bobby's. How many minutes would it take George to finish a 10-mile race?

(A) 300
(B) 600
(C) 500
(D) 150

Problem 115 (Word, Arithmetic Skills)

There are 60 brownies in a box to be distributed in a 1:2:4:5 ratio among four children. What is the second largest number of brownies that any one child can receive?

(A) 10
(B) 5
(C) 50
(D) 20

Problem 116 (Word, Geometry)

What is the area of a square obtained by joining two congruent triangles, given that the longest side of each triangle is $4\sqrt{3}$?

(A) 24
(B) 36
(C) 16
(D) $16\sqrt{3}$

Problem 117 (Arithmetic Skills)

If *N* and *M* are single-digit integers used to represent the numbers 18*N*, *N*5, and 1*M*9, calculate *M* given that

$$18N - N5 = 1M9$$

(A) 4
(B) 3
(C) 9
(D) 8

Problem 118 (Word, Arithmetic Skills)

A student planned to spend an hour and a half working on the homework for three subject areas: math, social studies, and science. If $\frac{1}{3}$ of this time was used for the math homework and $\frac{1}{4}$ of the *remaining* time is used for the social studies project, how many minutes does the student have left for his science homework?

(A) 20
(B) 35
(C) 45
(D) 55

8.2: Easy Problems; Open-Ended

Problem 119 (Word, Miscellaneous)

Michelle gets to keep a marble she will choose at random from a jar. The jar contains 23 white, 15 black, and 37 yellow marbles. Calculate the probability that Michelle picks out a black marble.

Problem 120 (Word, Arithmetic Skills)

300, 150, 75, 226, 113, 340, 170, . . .

Calculate the 10th term of the sequence above given that its first term is 300 and each term thereafter is obtained (1) dividing by 2, if the previous term is even, or (2) multiplying by 3 and then adding 1, if the previous term is odd.

Problem 121 (Word, Miscellaneous)

In a small town, a member of the Board of Education resigned and a new member was appointed. As a result, the ages of 8 of the 9 members are: 54, 66, 49, 57, 59, 62, 55, and 63. The youngest member of the new board happens to be 25 years younger than the oldest member. If the median age of the members is 57, what is the age of the newly appointed board member?

Problem 122 (Word, Geometry)

In a right triangle, the difference between the measures of the two smaller angles is 30°. Calculate the measure (in degrees) of the largest of the two angles.

Problem 123 (Word, Algebra)

The number of bears in a national park has tripled during every 3-year period because the beginning of 2000. If there were 8,100 bears in the park at the beginning of 2009, how many bears were in the same park at the beginning of 2000?

Problem 124 (Word, Geometry)

The clay needed to make a brick is contained in a spherical ball of clay with a radius of 3 inches. If a spherical ball of clay with a radius equal to 9 inches is delivered to the brick factory, how many bricks can be made out of it—given that the volume (V) of a sphere with radius r is given by the following formula:

$$V = \frac{4}{3}\pi r^3$$

Problem 125 (Word, Arithmetic Skills)

Grades are often computed using a weighted average. Suppose that home-work counts 5%, quizzes 15%, and tests 80%. Calculate a student's overall grade if his or her average/total grades in homework, quizzes, and tests were 70, 80, and 90, respectively.

Problem 126 (Word, Geometry)

In the figure below, $AB = 7$, $AD = 4$, $DC = 10$. What is the perimeter of the trapezoid $ABCD$?

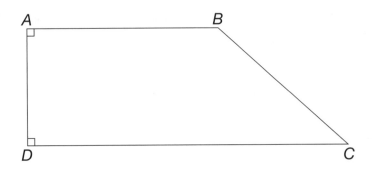

Note: Figure not drawn to scale.

8.3: Medium Problems; Multiple Choice

Problem 127 (Word, Arithmetic Skills)

In a clock factory, Mike assembles—on the average—15 clocks while his more experienced colleague, Steve, assembles 24 clocks in an hour. If the two workers were assigned two identical orders of 48 clocks, how many more minutes does it take Mike to assemble the clocks than it takes Steve?

(A) 48
(B) 72
(C) 24
(D) 15

Problem 128 (Word, Algebra)

In a metropolitan area, the standard charge for a speeding ticket is $60. An additional $10 charge is added for every mile per hour a driver travels above the speed limit. On a street where the speed limit was 30 miles per hour, a driver was fined $250 for speeding. Calculate the speed recorded by the police radar.

(A) 54
(B) 65
(C) 50
(D) 49

Problem 129 (Word, Miscellaneous)

At a used-camera shop, a customer could choose among 12 digital cameras of a certain brand. Nine of them were in perfect condition and 3 were defective or slightly damaged. The customer picked a camera that was supposed to be in perfect condition but shortly thereafter discovered that it was scratched. What is the probability that the second camera chosen is in perfect condition?

(A) $\dfrac{9}{11}$

(B) $\dfrac{8}{12}$

(C) $\dfrac{3}{11}$

(D) $\dfrac{8}{11}$

Problem 130 (Word, Algebra, Arithmetic Skills)

An auto plant in Michigan—currently under construction—is predicted to manufacture approximately 5 million cars in 2025. This number represents a 25% increase from the previous year. Which of the following best describes the number of cars manufactured in 2024?

(A) 1.25 million
(B) 2 million
(C) 4 million
(D) 5.25 million

Problem 131 (Word, Arithmetic Skills)

Samantha's choice for a four-digit number to be her computer password met the following rules:

*   the last digit had to be a divisor of 30
*   the greatest common factor of the middle two digits had to be 2
*   the leftmost/first digit was a prime number.

Which of the following numbers could be Samantha's password?

(A) 1216
(B) 2687
(C) 7466
(D) 5863

Problem 132 (Word, Algebra)

A bag contains blue, white, and red marbles. The number of white marbles is 2 more than the number of blue marbles, and the number of red marbles is 4 times the number of white marbles. Which of the following could be the total number of marbles in the bag?

(A) 53
(B) 48
(C) 26
(D) 46

Problem 133 (Word, Miscellaneous)

Three years ago, the average (arithmetic mean) number of rare coins owned by 20 collectors was 90. Today, 3 collectors updated their numbers as in the past 3 years, they acquired additional coins. The original numbers, 65, 58, and 55, were replaced by 85, 88, and 105, respectively. Calculate the correct average number of rare coins owned by the 20 collectors today.

(A) 85
(B) 105
(C) 100
(D) 95

Problem 134 (Word, Arithmetic Skills)

An ice-cream shop offers 6 different toppings for its ice cream cakes. The regular/standard price includes 2 different combinations. Calculate how many different combinations of toppings are available for no additional cost.

(A) 12
(B) 15
(C) 36
(D) 6

Problem 135 (Arithmetic Skills)

If $x^2 - y^2 = 55$ and $x - y = 5$, what is the value of y?

(A) 8
(B) 11
(C) 3
(D) 6

Problem 136 (Algebra)

Let the operation Δ be defined as $x \Delta y = x + 2xy - y$. How much greater is $5 \Delta 7$ than $3 \Delta 4$?

(A) 38
(B) 45
(C) 23
(D) 6

Problem 137 (Arithmetic Skills)

If x and y are odd integers, which of the following is NOT an odd integer?

   I. $(x-1)(y+2)$
   II. $(x+1) + 2y - 1$
   III. $(x-1) - y$

(A) I only
(B) II only
(C) III only
(D) I and II

Problem 138 (Miscellaneous)

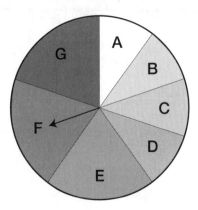

In the figure above, the regions A, B, C, and D have an equal area. Each of the equal regions E, F and G has twice the area of each of the equal regions A, B, C, and D. What is the probability that the tip of a spinner would stop at random in the F region?

(A) $\dfrac{1}{12}$

(B) $\dfrac{1}{5}$

(C) $\dfrac{1}{7}$

(D) $\dfrac{2}{7}$

Problem 139 (Algebra)

In the xy-plane, the line with equation $y = 7x - 28$ crosses the x-axis at the point with coordinates (a, b). What is the value of a?

(A) −28

(B) −2

(C) 0

(D) 4

Problem 140 (Algebra)

If $f(x) = 4 + 2x^2$, find the value of a positive integer k for which $f(2k) = 18k$

(A) −2
(B) 0
(C) 1
(D) 2

Problem 141 (Algebra)

There are 75 more men than women enrolled in a college. If the total number of student enrolled is 225, what percent of the students enrolled are women?

(A) 20%
(B) 33.33%
(C) 50%
(D) 66.66%

Problem 142 (Geometry)

The area of a rectangle is 125. What is its perimeter given that it can be divided into five equal squares?

(A) 25
(B) 60
(C) 75
(D) 50

Problem 143 (Algebra)

If $2x + 3$ is 5 less than $2y - 6$, calculate by what amount $x - 4$ is less than y.

(A) 16
(B) 8
(C) 13
(D) 11

Problem 144 (Algebra)

By definition, $(x)^* = 2x^2 - 3$. Find an expression for $[(y - z)^*] - [(y + z)^*]$.

(A) $-8yz$
(B) $8yz$
(C) $y^2 - z^2$
(D) $2y^2 + 2z^2$

Problem 145 (Arithmetic Skills)

30 less than 20% of 500 is equal to a number increased by 40% of its value. Calculate the number in question.

(A) 70
(B) 45
(C) 80
(D) 50

Problem 146 (Geometry)

The slope of a line is $\frac{1}{2}$. Calculate a if the line passes through points (0, *a*) and (2*a*, 1).

   (A) 1

   (B) 2

   (C) $\frac{1}{2}$

   (D) $-\frac{1}{2}$

Problem 147 (Word, Miscellaneous)

If Mike is *not* a member of the local swim and tennis club, indicate from which of the following statements it can be determined whether or not Mike is a member of the local golf club.

   (A) Some people who are not in the swim and tennis club are not in the golf club.

   (B) Anyone who is not in the swim and tennis club is not in the golf club.

   (C) No one is in both the swim and tennis club and the golf club.

   (D) Everyone in the swim and tennis club is in the golf club.

Problem 148 (Word, Miscellaneous)

On the playground of a nursery school, there is a box containing building blocks of different colors and shapes. If all of the cubes are blue, which of the following statements must be true?

I.   If a block is blue, then it is a cube.
II. If a block is not a cube, then it is not blue.
III. If a block is not blue, then it is not a cube.

(A) I only
(B) I and III only
(C) III only
(D) II only

Problem 149 (Word, Arithmetic Skills)

Pairs of Sneakers

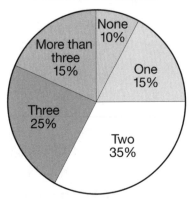

The figure above shows the percentages of players in a basketball camp who own the indicated number of sneakers. If 80 players own at least three pairs of sneakers, how many players own one pair or less?

(A) 80
(B) 48
(C) 52
(D) 50

Problem 150 (Word, Miscellaneous)

Consider the sequence

$$3, 9, 27, \ldots$$

Its first term is 3, and each term thereafter is three times the preceding term—making this a *geometric* sequence. Calculate the kth term of the sequence.

(A) $3k$

(B) k^2

(C) 3^k

(D) 3^{k-1}

Problem 151 (Word, Miscellaneous)

Calculate the average value of 25, a, b, 31, c, and d if the arithmetic mean of a and c is 15 and that of b and d is 23.

(A) 23

(B) 25

(C) 16

(D) 22

Problem 152 (Word, Arithmetic Skills)

The average (arithmetic mean) score received by a team of 15 members at a school competition was 87. When 5 additional members were added to the group, the average score of the team of 20 became 90. What is the average score of the 5 additional members to the team?

(A) 100

(B) 99

(C) 95

(D) 90

Problem 153 (Word, Algebra)

Let three numbers be *a*, *b*, and *c*. Their average is 2 less than 5 times the median. Calculate an expression for the average of *a* and *c* in terms of *b* given that $0 < a < b < c$.

(A) $7b - 3$

(B) $\dfrac{7b - 3}{2}$

(C) $5b - 2$

(D) $\dfrac{5b - 3}{2}$

Problem 154 (Word, Geometry)

The degree measures of the interior angles in a triangle are *x*°, 2*x*°, and 90°. Its longest leg is 20. What is the length of the leg opposing the angle with degree measure 2*x*°?

(A) $20\sqrt{3}$

(B) $10\sqrt{3}$

(C) 15

(D) 10

8.4: Medium Problems; Open-Ended

Problem 155 (Word, Algebra)

Lara and Matt borrowed 45 books from the library and had to return them the next day. If Lara returns 5 fewer books than four times as many books as Matt does, calculate the number of books Matt returns.

Problem 156 (Word, Miscellaneous)

The average (arithmetic mean) of five integers is the same as the median of the same numbers. If four of the five numbers are

$$13, 1, 7, 11$$

and the 5th is x, calculate all possible values for x.

Problem 157 (Word, Arithmetic Skills)

Each term after the second term of a sequence is the product of the two preceding terms. If the fifth and sixth terms are 16 and 256, respectively, calculate the first term of the sequence.

Problem 158 (Word, Arithmetic Skills)

A cafeteria has a lunch special consisting of soup or salad; a sandwich, coffee, tea, or one of three nonalcoholic beverages; and a dessert. If the menu lists 3 soups, 2 salads, 8 sandwiches, and 5 desserts, how many different lunches can one choose?

Problem 159 (Arithmetic Skills, Algebra)

$$1 \qquad k \qquad k+1 \qquad k+(k+1) \qquad \ldots$$

The first two terms in the sequence above are 1 and k, and each term thereafter is the sum of the two preceding terms. If the sum of the first 6 terms is 116, what is the value of k?

Problem 160 (Geometry)

In rectangle $ABCD$ below, $\dfrac{AG}{GD} = \dfrac{1}{3}$ and $\dfrac{DE}{DC} = \dfrac{3}{4}$. What is the value of the ratio

$$\frac{\text{Area}_{ABCD}}{\text{Area}_{DEFG}}?$$

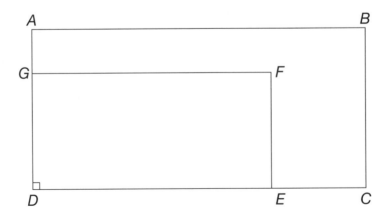

Note: Figure not drawn to scale.

Problem 161 (Word, Geometry)

A certain triangle has two angles with the same degree measure. If the lengths of two sides of the triangle are 5 and 7, what is the maximum value for the perimeter of the triangle?

Problem 162 (Word, Arithmetic Skills, Algebra)

At the end of the season, team A won $\frac{2}{5}$ and lost $\frac{1}{7}$ of the games it played against team B. During the entire season, the teams were tied in 32 games. Calculate the total number of games the teams played against each other.

Problem 163 (Word, Miscellaneous)

In Angelo's Restaurant, the daily menu featured 4 kinds of omelets. The first kind were made with 4 eggs each and they represented $\frac{1}{4}$ of the total number. The second kind used only 3 eggs each and they represented $\frac{2}{3}$ of the rest of the omelets. The remaining 80 omelets were equally split between the last two categories and only used 2 eggs each. Calculate the total number of eggs Angelo needs to make a daily supply of omelets.

Problem 164 (Word, Miscellaneous)

Seven friends played two rounds of a board game and each time accumulated an integer score. The two scores for each player were added together and the resulting numbers were 86, 98, 59, 48, 68, 72, and x. The seventh player, whose total score was x, obtained a score of 40 in the first round. Calculate one possible value of the seventh player's second-round score, given that x is the median of the seven total scores.

Problem 165 (Word, Miscellaneous)

A jar contains 15 red and 15 blue marbles. Calculate the least number of marbles that would have to be removed from the jar such that the ratio of blue to red marbles left in the jar will be 2 to 3.

Problem 166 (Word, Algebra)

Jane has four times as many marbles as Mike. If Jane gives Mike eight marbles, she will be left with four fewer marbles than him. What is the total number of marbles that Jane and Mike have?

Problem 167 (Word, Algebra)

Given three consecutive integers, if the sum of the first and third integers is increased by 8, the result is 5 less than triple the second integer. Find the first of the three consecutive integers.

Problem 168 (Word, Miscellaneous)

At a parent-teacher association meeting, the ratio of women to men is 3 to 5. Six women had to leave the meeting earlier and, as a result, the ratio of women to men becomes 1 to 2. How many women are in the room at the end of the meeting?

Problem 169 (Word, Algebra)

Anna joined her best friend and her family on a day trip and spent 30% and 45% of her daily allowance on breakfast and lunch, respectively. As a result, she's left with $15 to cover her dinner. How much money did she spend for breakfast?

8.5: Hard Problems; Multiple Choice

Problem 170 (Word, Miscellaneous)

The president of a college decided to retire in December 2009. He served in that capacity for 11 consecutive complete terms. Given that one complete term lasts 4 years—from the beginning of January of the first year through the end of December of the fourth year—calculate the year in which the president began to serve his first term.

(A) 1966
(B) 1965
(C) 1955
(D) 1956

Problem 171 (Word, Geometry)

In isosceles triangle ABC, side $\overline{BC}$ is longer than the other two sides. If the degree measure of $\angle A$ is a multiple of 22, calculate the greatest possible measure of $\angle C$.

(A) 78
(B) 88
(C) 75
(D) 79

Problem 172 (Word, Algebra)

A certain call—lasting more than a minute—costs $1.23. The telephone company calculates the charges according to the following formula: first minute costs m cents; each additional minute costs n cents. Of the expressions shown below, identify the one representing the length in minutes of the $1.23 call.

(A) $\dfrac{123-m}{n}$

(B) $\dfrac{123-m+n}{n}$

(C) $\dfrac{123}{m+n}$

(D) $\dfrac{123+m-n}{n}$

Problem 173 (Word, Arithmetic Skills)

Two sets of numbers, X and Y, are defined as the set of prime numbers and the set of two-digit, positive integers whose unit digit is 5, respectively. Calculate how many numbers are common to both sets.

(A) 0
(B) 2
(C) 3
(D) 1

Problem 174 (Word, Algebra)

x is a positive, odd integer. Calculate 20% of the value of the expression $3x + 8$, given that it satisfies the following double inequality:

$$60 < 3x + 8 < 70$$

(A) 52
(B) 57
(C) 13
(D) 60

Problem 175 (Word, Geometry)

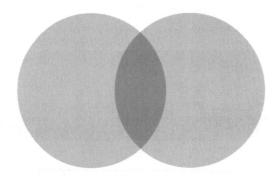

Two identical 300-degree arcs are joined together to enclose the area shown in the figure above (not drawn to scale). Both arcs are part of identical circles with radius equal to 12. Calculate the area of the shape shown in the figure.

(A) $120\pi + 72\sqrt{3}$
(B) $240\pi + 72\sqrt{3}$
(C) $240\pi + 36\sqrt{3}$
(D) $300\pi + 60\sqrt{3}$

Problem 176 (Word, Arithmetic Skills)

Consider a geometric sequence of positive numbers. After the first term, the ratio of each term to the term immediately preceding it is 3 to 1. Calculate the ratio of the ninth term in this sequence to the sixth term.

(A) 9:1
(B) 27:1
(C) 81:1
(D) 243:1

Problem 177 (Algebra)

Express 7^{3z+2} in terms of n, given that $7^z = n$?

(A) $7n^3$
(B) $49n$
(C) $49n^3$
(D) $49n^2$

Problem 178 (Word, Miscellaneous)

Two numbers, a and b, are selected at random from the set A and B, respectively, where

$$A = \{2, 5\}$$
$$B = \{1, 3, 6\}$$

Indicate which of the following statements must be true.

I.   The probability that $a + b$ is a prime number is $\dfrac{1}{2}$

II. The probability that $a + b > 8$ is $\dfrac{5}{6}$

III. The probability that $ab > a + b$ is $\dfrac{1}{3}$

(A) I only
(B) II only
(C) I and II only
(D) I and III only

Problem 179 (Word, Miscellaneous)

Four cheetahs were brought to a national park in an effort to reverse their extinction. At the time this experiment started, there were none left in the park. Through the care of the rangers, it is expected that this population will double its size every 5 years. Assuming the trend continues, how many more cheetahs will be in the park after 25 years than are in the park after 15 years?

(A) 24
(B) 300
(C) 96
(D) 100

Problem 180 (Algebra)

Calculate the values of x for which the expression $\dfrac{2x^2 - 3x + 9}{x^2 + x - 6}$ is undefined.

(A) 0, 6
(B) −3, 2
(C) −2, 3
(D) 0, 2

Problem 181 (Algebra)

Calculate the range of function $f(x) = 3x^2 - 5$ given that its domain of definition is restricted to $-1 \le x \le 7$.

(A) $-1 \le f(x) \le 142$
(B) $-5 \le f(x) \le 43$
(C) $-1 \le f(x) \le 43$
(D) $-5 \le f(x) \le 142$

8.6: Hard Problems; Open-Ended

Problem 182 (Word, Geometry)

Two triangles, T1 and T2, have sides of lengths 15 and 25. The length of the third side of each triangle is an integer. Calculate the greatest possible difference between the perimeters of the triangles T1 and T2.

Problem 183 (Word, Algebra)

Let A be a set consisting of n integers such that the difference between the greatest and the least integers is 225. Consider a second set of integers, B, formed by multiplying each integer in A by 6 and then subtracting 7 from the product. Calculate the difference between the greatest and the least integer in B.

Problem 184 (Word, Miscellaneous)

An opaque jar contains 5 red, 4 yellow, and 6 green candies. A child is allowed to pick two candies. What is the probability (1) of getting a green followed by a red candy or (2) of getting a red followed by a green or a yellow candy?

Problem 185 (Word, Geometry)

Lines *l* and *n* are parallel and their equations are: $3x - 2y = 8$ and $y = mx + b$ respectively. Knowing that in the *xy*-plane, line *n* passes through the point $(-1, 2)$, calculate the value of $m + b$.

Problem 186 (Word, Arithmetic Skills)

N and *a* are positive integers. Knowing that
1. $N = a^3$ and
2. *N* is divisible by 15 and 20,

calculate the smallest possible value of *N*.

Problem 187 (Geometry, Arithmetic Skills)

By what percent will the area of a circle increase, if its radius is quadrupled?

Problem 188 (Word, Geometry, Algebra)

Calculate the greatest possible perimeter of a triangle when the lengths of two of its sides are 7 and 11 and given that the third side is also an integer.

Problem 189 (Word, Miscellaneous)

In a class of 25 students, the average score on a final test calculated for 20 students was 75. Five students missed the test day with cold symptoms and were scheduled for a make-up. Their average score was eventually 80. What is the average score of the class?

Chapter

Solutions to Problems in Chapter 8

There are things which seem incredible to most
men who have not studied mathematics.

—Archimedes

Solution 90: A

The number of people expected on Sunday =
$$2(120-85)(85-75) = 2 \times 35 \times 10 = 700$$

The number of people expected on Saturday =
$$2(120-80)(80-75) = 2 \times 40 \times 5 = 400$$

The difference is $700 - 400 = 300$.

Solution 91: B

Translating English to Algebra, one can write:
$$x = 2yz - 7$$

Solution 92: D

The total number of assignments is
$$15 \times 4 + 3 \times 5 + 5 \times 1 = 60 + 15 + 5 = 80$$

Solution 93: C

No matter how the two circles are positioned, it is easy to observe that they can have 0 (no overlap), 1 (they are tangent), or 2 (maximum) number of points of intersection.

Solution 94: D

Given that the third angle whose measure is not shown in the figure is congruent with b (vertical angles) and that $a° = 58°$, one can write:
$$b° = 180° - (a° + 72°) = 180° - 130° = 50°$$

Solution 95: D

If he completes 1 lap in 15 minutes, in 6 minutes he will cover "x of a lap," or you can set up the problem like this:

$$15 \text{ min} \ldots\ldots\ldots 1 \text{ [lap]}$$
$$6 \text{ min} \ldots\ldots\ldots x \text{ [lap]}$$

where (after cross multiplication)
$$x = \frac{6}{15} = \frac{2}{5} \text{ [of a lap]}.$$

Solution 96: A

The price of a tomato is equal to the total price (d) divided by the total number of tomatoes purchased, or t (number of tomatoes in a box) multiplied by b (total number of boxes):
$$\frac{d}{bt}$$

Solution 97: B

Substituting 2 for x and y leads to:
$$2^3 \times 2^2 = 8 \times 4 = 32$$

Solution 98: A

The product $2x$ must be a multiple of 7. The only value that meets this requirement is $x = -14$ in which case
$$\frac{2x}{7} = -4 = \text{a negative integer}$$

Solution 99: C

In ascending order, positive odd integers are:
$$1, 3, 5, 7, 9, \ldots$$

Three times an odd (positive) integer gives us:
$$3, 9, 15, 21, 27, \ldots$$

As a result, the number of positive integers that satisfies the requirement is 4 (i.e., 3, 9, 15, and 21).

Solution 100: A

The sum of the interior angle measures in a quadrilateral is 360°. Subtracting the degree measure of the fourth angle gives us the sum of the remaining three to be:
$$360° - 60° = 300°$$

Given that the degree measures of the remaining three angles are in the ratio 2:3:5 and that their sum is 300°, the measures of the angles in question are $\frac{300°}{(2+3+5)} = 30°$ multiplied by 2, 3, and 5, respectively:
$$60°, 90°, \text{ and } 150°.$$

The measure of the largest angle is therefore 150°.

Solution 101: D

Remember: 1ft = 12 in

The area to be covered in in² is
$$1 \times 12 \times 2 \times 12 = 288 \ [in^2]$$

The area of a tile is
$$4 \times 4 = 16 \ [in^2]$$

The number of tiles needed is therefore
$$\frac{288}{16} = 18$$

Solution 102: B

First we eliminate the choices that are odd numbers (because they are not divisible by 2), or A and C.

Of the remaining two, division by 3 gives us a remainder of 1 (B) or 0 (D).

The answer is therefore B.

Solution 103: D

Substituting 2 for x in the first equation gives us $y = 4$. Furthermore, substituting 2 and 4 for x and y, respectively, in the expression we need to calculate leads to
$$2^2(4-1) = 4 \times 3 = 12$$

Solution 104: D

25% of the total number of students (i.e., $16 + 8 = 24$) equals the number of boys who were present:
$$\frac{25}{100} \times 24 = 6$$

The total number of boys who missed school that day was therefore:
$$16 - 6 = 10$$

Solution 105: D

Because line *l* is perpendicular to the *y*-axis and therefore parallel to the *x*-axis, any point that belongs to it will have a *y* coordinate of 6. The only answer that matches this requirement is (2, 6).

Solution 106: C

$729 = 3^6$ therefore $3^{2x} = 3^6$

When two powers of the same base are equal, the exponents must also be equal, therefore $2x = 6$ which means that $x = 3$.

Solution 107: A

Out of 250 pigeons that were released, $250 - 50 = 200$ reached the destination. The ratio of them over the total number of pigeons released is

$$\frac{200}{250} = \frac{4}{5}$$

Solution 108: C

Let *x* and *y* be the lengths of the longer and shorter piece of tape, respectively. It follows that

$$x = 3y + 8 = 56$$

or

$$3y = (56 - 8) = 48$$

or

$$y = \frac{48}{3} = 16$$

Solution 109: D

From the tables: $\$240 \times 80 + \$25 \times 200 = \$19{,}200 + \$5{,}000 = \$24{,}200$

Solution 110: C

This problem is a simple test of your analytic/critical thinking and reading comprehension skills. Using the requirements stated in the problem, one concludes that the houses marked with an "X" cannot be painted gray.

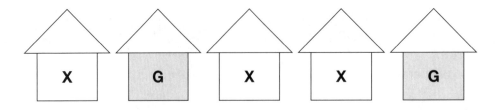

Eastside Blvd.

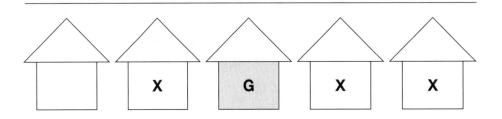

As a result, there is only one house left that can be painted gray. The answer is therefore "1" or C.

Solution 111: C

If you multiply the first equation by 2 and add it to the second equation, terms containing "y" will cancel out:

$$4x - 2y = 14$$
$$3x + 2y = 35$$
$$\overline{}$$
$$7x = 49$$
or
$$x = 7$$

Solution 112: C

This is a logic problem and one way to solve it would be to come up with a notation to list the kids' ages in ascending order; for example, one can use the symbol ">" to denote that someone's age is greater than somebody else's (and, by the same token, "<" is used to denote that someone's age is less than somebody else's); for example:

$$\text{Monica} > \text{John} > \text{Briana}$$
$$\text{Luke} > \text{John}$$

By comparing each statement with the two above, we can easily eliminate all statements except the one that corresponds to Luke > Briana, or C.

Solution 113: A

$$3a - 2b = 4b \text{ or } 3a = 6b$$
$$2b = 3 \text{ or } 6b = 9 \text{ thus } 3a = 9 \text{ or } a = 3$$
$$5a = 5 \times 3 = 15$$

Solution 114: B

Bobby's rate is

$$\frac{15}{3} = 5 \left[\frac{\text{miles}}{\text{hour}}\right]$$

and therefore George's rate is

$$\frac{5}{5} = 1 \left[\frac{\text{mile}}{\text{hour}}\right].$$

As a result, it would take George

$$\frac{10 \left[\text{miles}\right]}{1 \left[\dfrac{\text{mile}}{\text{hour}}\right]} = 10 \text{ [hours] or } 10 \times 60 = 600 \text{ [minutes]}$$

to complete his race.

Solution 115: D

If the smallest number of brownies distributed is x, one can write the equation:

$$x + 2x + 4x + 5x = 12\ x = 60 \text{ or } x = \frac{60}{12} = 5$$

to represent the distribution based on the given ratios.

As a result, the four children will receive—in ascending order—5, 10, 20, and 25 brownies. The second largest number of brownies received is therefore 20.

Solution 116: A

In order for two congruent triangles to fit together and form a square, they would have to be right isosceles triangles joined at the hypotenuse. The legs of the triangles would form the sides of the square all equal to—say—"a," with the longest side of the triangles being the diagonal of the square. As a result, applying the Pythagorean Theorem, we have the following equation:

$$a^2 + a^2 = (4\sqrt{3})^2 \text{ or } 2a^2 = 16 \times 3 \text{ or } a^2 = 24$$

Solution 117: B

N and M represent the unit's and ten's digits. We can rewrite the terms of the equation above as follows:

$$18N = 100 + 80 + N$$

$$N5 = 10 \times N + 5$$

$$1M9 = 100 + 10 \times M + 9$$

or

$$100 + 80 + N - 10 \times N - 5 = 100 + 10 \times M + 9$$

or

$$66 = 10 \times M + 9 \times N$$

The only digit that multiplied by 9 gives you a number that ends in 6 is 4, therefore $N = 4$ and $10 \times M = 30$ or $M = 3$.

Solution 118: C

The student spends 30 minutes working on the math homework, which represents $\frac{1}{3}$ of the 90 minutes available. The remaining time to work on the other two subjects is 60 minutes. $\frac{1}{4}$ of it represents the 15 minutes spent on the social studies homework. Therefore, there are 45 minutes left for the science homework.

Solution 119: 1/5 or 0.2

The probability that Michelle chose a black marble is equal to the number of black marbles divided by the total number of marbles in the jar:

$$\frac{15}{(23+15+37)} = \frac{15}{75} = \frac{1}{5} = 0.2$$

Solution 120: 128

The eighth term: $\frac{170}{2} = 85$

The ninth term: $3 \times 85 + 1 = 256$

The 10th term: $\frac{256}{2} = 128$

Solution 121: 41

Let's first arrange the numbers in ascending order:

$$49, 54, 55, 57, 59, 62, 63, 66$$

Given that the median age of all 9 members is 57 and four ages are greater and three less than that, the age of the newly elected member must be less than 57, which means that the oldest member is 66. As a result, the youngest member's age is $66 - 25 = 41$ and because this age is not equal to any of the ages of the known members, it follows that the age of the new member must be 41.

Solution 122: 60°

Let the degree measures of the two smaller angles be S and L, where $L > S$. It follows that

$$L + S = 90° \text{ and } S = L - 30° \text{ or}$$
$$L + L - 30° = 90° \text{ or}$$
$$L = \frac{(90° + 30)}{2} = 60°$$

Solution 123: 300

Let "x" be the numbers of bears at the beginning of year 2000. It follows that the numbers of bears at the beginning of 2003, 2006, and 2009 were $3x$, $9x$, and $27x$, respectively. If $27x = 8,100$ then the number of bears at the beginning of 2000 is $x = \dfrac{8,100}{27} = 300$.

Solution 124: 27

The ratio of the two volumes is

$$\frac{9^3}{3^3} = 3^3 = 27$$

Solution 125: 87.5

The student's overall grade $= 0.05 \times 70 + 0.15 \times 80 + 0.80 \times 90 = 87.5$

Solution 126: 26

The perimeter of $ABCD$ is the sum of its sides,
$$P_{ABCD} = AB + BC + CD + AD$$

The only side that is not given is BC, but it can be derived by applying the Pythagorean Theorem in right triangle BCE drawn below:

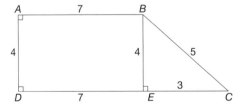

$$
\begin{aligned}
EC &= DC - AB = 10 - 7 = 3 \\
BE &= AD = 4 \\
BC^2 &= BE^2 + EC^2 \\
BC^2 &= 4^2 + 3^2 = 16 + 9 = 25 \\
BC &= 5 \\
P_{ABCD} &= AB + BC + CD + AD = 7 + 5 + 10 + 4 = 26
\end{aligned}
$$

Solution 127: B

To assemble 48 clocks, Mike needs $\dfrac{(48 \times 60)}{15} = 192$ [minutes] while Steve completes the order in $\dfrac{(48 \times 60)}{24} = 120$ [minutes]. As a result, Steve needs $192 - 120 = 72$ more minutes.

Solution 128: D

Assume the speed of the car was "x" [miles/hour] where $x > 30$ (otherwise, the fine would have been equal with the standard charge of \$60). We can then express the amount of the fine as given by the following formula:
$$250 = 60 + 10(x - 30)$$

Where "$x - 30$" represents the number of miles over the speed limit for which the driver had to pay an extra \$10.

Solving for x gives us
$$190 = 10x - 300 \text{ or } 10x = 490 \text{ and thus } x = \frac{490}{10} = 49 \left[\frac{\text{miles}}{\text{hour}}\right]$$

Solution 129: D

The probability of a camera picked at random to be in perfect condition is
$$\frac{\text{total number of cameras in perfect condition}}{\text{total number of cameras}} = \frac{9}{12} = \frac{3}{4}$$

The same probability after a camera initially listed to be in perfect condition was removed from the mix is
$$\frac{\text{total number of cameras in perfect condition left}}{\text{total number of cameras left}} = \frac{8}{11}$$

Solution 130: C

Let x be the number of cars built in 2024 and—as a reference—this number represents 100%. The number of cars built in 2025—compared to x—is 25% more, thus it represents 125% of x and is equal to 5 million. As a result,

$$\frac{125x}{100} = 5 \text{ [million] or } x = \frac{500}{125} = \frac{20}{5} = 4 \text{ [million]}$$

Solution 131: D

First condition rules out (B). Second condition rules out (A). We're left with either (C) or (D), but the third condition is only true for (D).

Solution 132: D

Let B, W, and R be the numbers of blue, white, and red marbles, respectively. With these notations, translating English to algebra leads to the following equations:

$$W = B + 2 \text{ and } R = 4W$$

Substituting "$B + 2$" for W and "$4(B + 2)$" for R, we can now express the total number of marbles in terms of B, or

$$B + W + R = B + B + 2 + 4B + 8 = 6B + 10$$

Because B must be an integer, the only answer from which subtracting 10 will result in a number that's divisible by 6 is 46 or D.

Solution 133: D

The total number of coins owned by the 20 collectors has increased by

$$(85 + 88 + 105) - (65 + 58 + 55) = 278 = 178 = 100 \text{ [coins]}$$

As a result, the average/arithmetic mean has increased by

$$\frac{100}{20} = 5$$

And thus the new average is

$$90 + 5 = 95$$

Solution 134: B

Solution #1

Let's consider 6 different toppings denoted 1 through 6. The total combinations in which they can be served—given that their order is irrelevant—can be calculated as follows:

$$(1, 2)\ (1, 3)\ (1, 4)\ (1, 5)\ (1, 6)$$
$$(2, 3)\ (2, 4)\ (2, 5)\ (2, 6)$$
$$(3, 4)\ (3, 5)\ (3, 6)$$
$$(4, 5)\ (4, 6)$$
$$(5, 6)$$

for a total of 15.

Solution #2

The same result is obtained using the formula for "combinations" (see p. 73), or:

$$nC = \frac{nPr}{r!} = \frac{n!}{r!(n-r)!} = \frac{6!}{2!(6-2)!} = \frac{5 \times 6}{2} = 15$$

Solution 135: C

$x^2 - y^2$ can be decomposed as $(x - y)(x + y)$ and it equals to 55. Because $x - y = 5$, $x + y$ should be 11 (55 divided by 5). As a result, we have a system of two equations in x and y:

$$x - y = 5$$
$$x + y = 11$$

Adding the equations leads to

$$2x = 16$$

therefore $x = 8$ and (after substituting 8 for x in one of the two equations above)

$$y = 3$$

Solution 136: B

According to the definition of the operation Δ,
$$5 \Delta 7 = 5 + 2 \times 5 \times 7 - 7 = 5 + 70 - 7 = 68$$
$$3 \Delta 4 = 3 + 2 \times 3 \times 4 - 4 = 3 + 24 - 4 = 23$$

Therefore $(5 \Delta 7) - (3 \Delta 5) = 68 - 23 = 45$

Solution 137: A

Because x is an odd number, $x-1$ is an even number, which when multiplied by any other number results in an even number. Therefore expression I does not represent an odd integer.

Because x is an odd number, $x + 1$ is an even number, and $2y$ is also an even number, which makes $(x + 1) + 2y$ even, and $(x + 1) + 2y - 1$ odd, therefore statement II represents an odd number.

Expression III represents an odd number because x is odd, which makes $x-1$ even, and when an odd number y is subtracted from it, the result is again odd.

Solution 138: B

Each of the regions E, F, and G is the equivalent of 2 of the small regions A, B, C, or D. The entire circle consists of 4 small regions (A, B, C and D) and 3 double regions (E, F, G), in other words, the equivalent of $4 + 3 \times 2 = 10$ small regions. That counts for the total number of events. Out of these 10 regions, two of them are covered by the region F. In other words, two is the number of favorable events (outcomes) out of 10 total events possible. Therefore, the probability that the spinner would land on the region F is $\dfrac{2}{10}$ or $\dfrac{1}{5}$.

Solution 139: D

At the point where the line crosses the x-axis, the value of the y-coordinate in that point is 0; therefore, the coordinates (a, b) are in fact $(a, 0)$. A solution can be found by substituting them in the equation of the line and solving for a:
$$0 = 7a - 28$$
$$28 = 7a$$

$$a = \frac{28}{7}$$
$$a = 4$$

Solution 140: D

According to the definition of the function,
$$f(2k) = 4 + 2(2k)^2 = 4 + (2 \times 4k^2) = 4 + 8k^2 = 18k$$

Rearranging the terms of the last equation leads to
$$8k^2 - 18k + 4 = 0$$
$$8k^2 - 16k - 2k + 4 = 0$$
$$8k(k-2) - 2(k-2) = 0$$
$$(k-2)(8k-2) = 0$$
$$2(k-2)(4k-1) = 0$$

Of the two solutions, we pick the one that's an integer: $k = 2$.

Solution 141: B

Let w be the number of women enrolled. The number or men enrolled is therefore $w + 75$ and their sum adds up to the total number of student enrolled:
$$w + w + 75 = 225$$
$$2w + 75 = 225$$
$$2w = 225 - 75$$
$$2w = 150$$
$$w = 75$$

If P is the percentage of women enrolled,
$$75 = \frac{P}{100} \times 225$$

$$P = \frac{75 \times 100}{225} = 33.33\%$$

Solution 142: B

The five squares together make up the area of the rectangle and can only be positioned (given that it's an odd number) in a row.

The area of each square is $\dfrac{125}{5} = 25$ and one side of the squares is therefore $\sqrt{25} = 5$.

The length of the rectangle is $5 \times 5 = 25$ and the width is 5. As a result, its perimeter is

$$2 \times (25 + 5) = 60$$

Solution 143: D

Translating the problem into equations leads to:
$$2x + 3 = 2y - 6 - 5$$

or

$$2x = 2y - 14$$

or

$$x = y - 7$$

and

$$x - 4 = y - 7 - 4 = y - 11$$

Solution 144: A

Applying the definition of symbol * to the expression in question leads to
$$[(y-z)^*] - [(y + z)^*] = [2(y-z)^2 - 3] - [2(y + z)^2 - 3] =$$
$$2y^2 - 4yz + 2z^2 - 3 - 2y^2 - 4yz - 2z^2 + 3 =$$
$$-8yz$$

Solution 145: D

Let the number we need to calculate be N. Increasing it by 40% of its value gives us 140% of N or $1.4N$.

"30 less than 20% of 500" can be expressed as

$$\frac{20}{100} \times 500 - 30 = 70 = 1.4N$$

or

$$N = \frac{70}{1.4} = 50$$

Solution 146: C

The general equation of a line is $y = mx + b$ (where m = the slope and b = the y-intercept). Writing it twice to account for the two points through which the line passes leads to:

$$a = b$$
$$1 = a + b$$

or (after substituting a for b in the second equation)

$$a = \frac{1}{2}$$

Solution 147: B

Combining reading comprehension and logic skills, this problem is putting to test the student's analytic/critical thinking abilities. It turns out that the *only* statement from which one can determine with certitude (i.e., "must be" as opposed to "can/may be") whether Mike belongs to the golf club is B.

Solution 148: C

Combining reading comprehension and logic skills, this problem is putting to test the student's analytic/critical thinking abilities. To solve it, one needs to compare the statement "all of the cubes are blue" with the three statements numbered "I" through "III." After ruling out statements "I" and "II," one finds statement "III" as being fully compatible with the given statement.

Solution 149: D

Let the total number of players who registered for the camp be P. The percentage of players who own at least three pairs of sneakers is 25% + 15% = 40% of the total or 80 players. Thus, the total number of campers is

$$\frac{40}{100}P = 80 \ \text{ or } \ P = \frac{100 \times 80}{40} = 200$$

The percentage of players who own one pair or less is 15% + 10% = 25% and that translates into

$$\frac{25}{100} \times 200 = 50 \ \text{[players]}$$

Solution 150: C

The first term = 3; second term = $3 \times 3 = 3^2 = 9$; third term = $3^2 \times 3 = 3^3 = 27$. By extrapolating the observation that the rank/term is equal to the exponent (power of) 3, we find that the kth term = 3^k

Solution 151: D

The "arithmetic mean" or "average value" of a and c is 15 or $a + c = 15 \times 2 = 30$. Similarly, the average of b and d is 23 or $b + d = 23 \times 2 = 46$. Thus, $a + b + c + d = 76$ and the required arithmetic mean:

$$\frac{25 + a + b + 31 + c + d}{6} = \frac{25 + 76 + 31}{6} = \frac{132}{6} = 22$$

Solution 152: B

Let S_1 through S_{15} be the scores obtained by the original 15 members and S_{16} through S_{20} the scores obtained by the new members (5). Using the average formula, the following equations can be written:

$$87 = \frac{S_1 + S_2 + S_3 + \ldots + S_{13} + S_{14} + S_{15}}{15}$$

or

$$S_1 + S_2 + S_3 + \ldots + S_{13} + S_{14} + S_{15} = 87 \times 15 = 1305$$

$$90 = \frac{S_1 + S_2 + S_3 + \ldots + S_{13} + S_{14} + S_{15} + S_{16} + S_{17} + S_{18} + S_{19} + S_{20}}{20}$$

or (substituting the sum of the first 15 scores obtained above)

$$90 = \frac{1305 + S_{16} + S_{17} + S_{18} + S_{19} + S_{20}}{20}$$

$$1305 + S_{16} + S_{17} + S_{18} + S_{19} + S_{20} = 90 \times 20 = 1,800$$

$$S_{16} + S_{17} + S_{18} + S_{19} + S_{20} = 1,800 - 1,305 = 495$$

The average (arithmetic mean) of the new members of the team is the sum of their scores divided by 5 or

$$\frac{S_{16} + S_{17} + S_{18} + S_{19} + S_{20}}{5} = \frac{495}{5} = 99$$

Solution 153: A

Applying "translation of English to algebra" to the first two sentences leads to

$$\frac{a+b+c}{3} = 5b - 2$$

or

$$a + b + c = 15b - 6 \text{ or } a + c = 14b - 6$$

and therefore

$$\frac{a+c}{2} = 7b - 3$$

Solution 154: B

The sum of interior angles in the triangle is

$$180° = 90° + x° + 2x° = 90° + 3x°$$

or

$$x° = 30°$$

As a result, we are dealing with a "30-60-90" triangle which has side lengths in the ratio:

$$1 : \sqrt{3} : 2$$

or the side lengths are:

$$10, \ 10\sqrt{3}, \text{ and } 20$$

The length of the side opposing the 60° angle is therefore $10\sqrt{3}$

Solution 155: 10

Let L and M be the number of books borrowed/returned by Lara and Matt, respectively. With these notations, translating the English to algebra leads to the following equations:

$$L + M = 45$$
$$L = 4M - 5$$

Substituting $(4M - 5)$ for L in the first equation leads to:

$$4M - 5 + M = 45$$
$$5M = 50$$
$$M = 10$$

Solution 156: 3, 8, or 23

It helps to rearrange the numbers in ascending order: 1, 7, 11, 13

Solution #1

The average value of the five numbers is given by
$$\frac{13 + 1 + 7 + 11 + x}{5} = \frac{32 + x}{5}$$

Given that the result must equal one of the numbers, thus it must be an integer, $(32 + x)$ must be divisible by 5 or
$$x = 3, 8, 13, 18, 23, 28, \ldots$$

(an arithmetic series with first term = 3 and each subsequent one being equal to the previous + 5). The table below identifies the values of x that satisfy the requirement that the average value be equal to the median.

x	average	median
3	7	7
8	8	8
13	9	11
18	10	11
23	11	11
28	12	11

As a result, the solution is $x = 3$, 8, or 23.

Solution #2

Let the median value be M. Looking at possible values for x in the set arranged in ascending order and given that the relationship between x and M is

$$x = 5M - 32$$

we can identify three options.

a. $x < 7$ in which case $M = 7$
b. $7 < x < 11$ in which case $M = x$
c. $x > 11$ in which case $M = 11$

Substituting these values in the equation above leads to $x = 3$, 8, or 23.

Solution 157: 1/16

The fifth and sixth terms are 16 and 256, respectively, or 2^4 and 2^8.
Dividing the sixth term by the fifth term, one obtains the fourth term, or 2^4.
Dividing the fifth term by the fourth term, one obtains the third term, or 1.
Dividing the fourth term by the third term, one obtains the second term, or 2^4.
Dividing the third term by the second term, one obtains the first term, or
$2^{-4} = \dfrac{1}{16}$

Solution 158: 1,000

The group of 4 elements the combinations of which we need to calculate is:
soup/salad, sandwich, coffee/tea/beverage, dessert

The corresponding numbers involved in the combinations are
3/2, 8, 1/1/3, 5

The number of different lunches is
$$(3 + 2) \times 8 \times (1 + 1 + 3) \times 5 = 5 \times 8 \times 5 \times 5 = 1000$$

Solution 159: 9

The first 6 terms in the series are:

$$1 \qquad k \qquad k+1 \qquad 2k+1 \qquad 3k+2 \qquad 5k+3$$

Their sum is

$$1 + k + (k+1) + (2k+1) + (3k+2) + (5k+3) = 12k + 8 = 116$$

Solving the last line of the equation leads to

$$12k = 116 - 8$$
$$12k = 108$$
$$k = 9$$

Solution 160: 16/9 or 1.777

$$\text{Area}_{ABCD} = AD \times DC \text{ and Area}_{DEFG} = GD \times DE$$

The ratio of the two areas, $\dfrac{\text{Area}_{ABCD}}{\text{Area}_{DEFG}} = \dfrac{AD \times DC}{DE \times GD}$

If $\dfrac{AG}{GD} = \dfrac{1}{3}$ then because of the properties of proportions,

$$\frac{AG + GD}{GD} = \frac{AD}{GD}$$

$$\frac{1+3}{3} = \frac{4}{3}$$

The ratio of the areas can be therefore rewritten as

$$\frac{\text{Area}_{ABCD}}{\text{Area}_{DEFG}} = \frac{AD}{GD} \times \frac{DC}{DE} = \frac{4}{3} \times \frac{4}{3} = \frac{16}{9}$$

Solution 161: 19

Because two of its angles are equal, the triangle is isosceles. That means that two of its sides also have equal lengths. There are two possible options with respect to its perimeter:

5, 5, and 7 for which the perimeter (5 + 5 + 7) is 17

5, 7, and 7 for which the perimeter (5 + 7 + 7) is 19

The second option leads to the maximum perimeter, with a value of 19.

Solution 162: 70

Let X be the number of games the two teams played against each other during the whole season.

The fraction of games that resulted in a tie was

$$1 - \left(\frac{2}{5} + \frac{1}{7} \right) = \frac{35 - 14 - 5}{35} = \frac{16}{35}$$

or

$$\frac{16}{35} X = 32$$

or

$$X = \frac{35 \times 32}{16} = 70$$

Solution 163: 960

Let X be the total number of omelets. With this notation, we can write the following equations:

$$X = \frac{X}{4} + \frac{2}{3} \left(X - \frac{X}{4} \right) + 80$$

$$X = \frac{X}{4} + \frac{2}{3} \times \frac{3X}{4} + 80$$

$$X = \frac{X}{4} + \frac{X}{2} + 80$$

$$X = \frac{3X}{4} + 80$$

$$\frac{X}{4} = 80$$

$$X = 320$$

number of eggs used for first kind of omelet =

$$4 \times 320 \times \frac{1}{4} = 320 \times \frac{4}{4} = 320$$

number of eggs used for the second kind of omelet =

$$3 \times 320 \times \frac{3}{4} \times \frac{2}{3} = 320 \times \frac{3}{2} = 480$$

number of eggs used for the third and fourth kinds of omelet =
$$80 \times 2 = 160$$

or

$$\text{Total number of eggs} = 320 + 480 + 160 = 960$$

Solution 164: 28, 29, 30, 31, or 32

Let's rearrange the known total scores in ascending order, or
$$48, 59, 68, 72, 86, 98$$

It is easy to observe that for the total score of the seventh player—x—to also be the median of this series, the following double inequality would have to be satisfied:
$$68 \leq x \leq 72$$

Because if $x < 68$ or $x > 72$, the median would be 68 or 72, respectively. As a result, the acceptable range for the second score obtained by the seventh player is calculated by subtracting 40 from all of the terms of the double inequalities:
$$28 \leq x - 40 \leq 32$$

Solution 165: 5

In the end, the total number of marbles would represent 3 parts (red) plus 2 parts (blue) for a total of 5 parts of the jar content. As a result, that number would have to be divisible by 5 and to calculate "the least" number of marbles that would have to be removed from the jar, we have to consider the largest integer less than 30 (the initial total) that is divisible by 5. The result is 25, thus 5 marbles would have to be removed from the jar.

(Note that the jar will now contain $2 \times \dfrac{25}{5} = 10$ blue and $3 \times \dfrac{25}{5} = 15$ red marbles, or all of the marbles removed had to be blue.)

Solution 166: 20

Let the number of marbles originally in Jane's and Mike's possession be J and M, respectively.

Translation of the first sentence leads to:
$$J = 4 \times M$$

Translation of the second sentence leads to:
$$J - 8 = M + 8 - 4$$

We are now left with the easier task (after simplifying and rearranging the second equation in step #2) of solving the following set of equations:
$$J = 4 \times M$$
$$J = M + 12$$

Solving by substitution leads to $4M = M + 12$, or $3M = 12$, or
$$M = 4 \text{ and } J = 4 \times 4 = 16$$

The result $(J + M)$ is thus 20.

Solution 167: 12

Let the three consecutive integers be $x, x + 1, x + 2$. Translating the first sentence to algebra leads to:
$$x + (x + 2) + 8 = 3(x + 1) - 5 = 3x - 2$$
$$x = 12$$

Solution 168: 30

Let's denote by W and M the number of women and men initially attending the meeting.
$$\frac{W}{M} = \frac{3}{5}$$
Also
$$\frac{W - 6}{M} = \frac{1}{2}$$

Cross multiplication leads to the following equations:

$$5W = 3M$$
$$2W - 12 = M$$

Substituting the expression for M (second equation) into the first equation leads to

$$5W = 3(2W - 12) = 6W - 36 \text{ or } W = 36.$$

Because this is the initial number of women attending the meeting and 6 of them left earlier, the number of women in the room at the end of the meeting was $36 - 6 = 30$.

Solution 169: 18

If she spent 30% and 45% of her money for breakfast and lunch, she's left with $100\% - (30\% + 45\%) = 25\%$ to spend for dinner. That money represents $15, meaning that her daily allowance was $4 \times \$15 = \$60$.

Of that amount, she spent 30% for breakfast, or $\dfrac{30}{100} \times \$60 = \$18$.

Solution 170: A

The president's first year in office was

$$2009 - (4 \times 11) + 1 = 2010 - 44 = 1966$$

Solution 171: D

Given the configuration of the triangle (the two equal angles are B and C), the greatest possible measure of $\angle C$ is calculated considering the smallest possible value for the measure of $\angle A$, or 22°, thus

$$\text{Max } \angle C = \frac{180° - 22°}{2} = 79°$$

Solution 172: B

Let x be the length of the call expressed in minutes. Based on the information given to us, the total amount for the call—expressed in cents—can be calculated using the following equation:

$$123 = m + n(x-1) = m + nx - n$$

Rearranging the terms, one can write

$$x = \frac{123 - m + n}{n}$$

Solution 173: A

Based on the information given to us in the text of the problem, the two sets in question are

$$X: 2, 3, 5, 7, 11, 13, 17, \ldots$$
$$Y: 15, 25, 35, 45, 55, \ldots$$

The intersection of them leads to a set consisting of . . . no numbers!

Solution 174: C

The double inequality is satisfied by the following values for the expression $3x + 18$:

$$61, 62, 63, 64, 65, 66, 67, 68, 69$$

If we subtract 8, we end up with the following options as possible values for $3x$:

$$53, 54, 55, 56, 57, 58, 59, 60, 61$$

Given that x is an integer, the acceptable options are only those values that are divisible by 3:

$$54, 57, 60$$

and given that x is also an odd number, we end up with

$$3x = 57, \text{ or } 3x + 8 = 57 + 8 = 65.$$

The answer: 20% of $65 = \dfrac{65}{5} = 13$.

Another solution can be obtained starting with the double inequality

$$60 < 3x + 8 < 70 \text{ or}$$
$$52 < 3x < 62 \text{ or}$$

$$\frac{52}{3} < x < \frac{62}{3} \text{ or}$$

$$17\frac{1}{3} < x < 20\frac{2}{3}$$

And, given that x is a positive, odd integer, the only value that satisfies the above double inequality is 19 or $x = 19$. It follows that 20% of $(3x + 8)$ is

$$\frac{1}{5}(57 + 8) = \frac{1}{5} \times 65 = 13$$

Solution 175: B

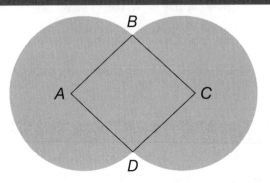

The area in question is the sum of two identical circle sectors with a central angle of 300° plus the area of the rhombus ($ABCD$) with sides equal to 12 (the circle radius) as illustrated above.

The area of a circle sector with a central angle equal to 300° is S, where

360°..............$\pi r^2 = 144\pi$

300°.........................S

_____

Cross multiplication leads to $S = 120\pi$

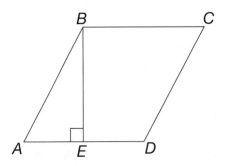

In the figure above, the measure of angle A is $360° - 300° = 60°$. Triangle ABE is a right triangle with angle measures of 30°, 60°, and 90°, respectively. As a result,

$$BE = \frac{\sqrt{3}}{2}AB = \frac{\sqrt{3}}{2} \times 12 = 6\sqrt{3}$$

and the area of the rhombus *ABCD* is

$$12 \times 6\sqrt{3} = 72\sqrt{3}$$

The requested area is therefore

$$2 \times 120\pi + 72\sqrt{3} = 240\pi + 72\sqrt{3}$$

Solution 176: B

Let the   first term $= x$

second term $= 3x$

third term $= 3^2 x$

fourth term $= 3^3 x$ . . . by extrapolation (the power = rank number -1)

or

sixth term $= 3^5 x$ and ninth term $= 3^8 x$

$$\frac{\text{ninth term}}{\text{sixth term}} = \frac{3^8}{3^5} = 3^3 = 27 \text{ or } 27:1$$

Solution 177: C

$$7^{3z+2} = 7^{3z} \times 7^2 = 49(7^z)^3 = 49n^3$$

The result is therefore C.

Solution 178: A

The following are all possible outcomes of selecting *a* and *b* randomly from sets *A* and *B*:

(2,1) (2, 3) (2,6) (5,1) (5,3) (5,6)

The possible outcome for $a + b$ is

3, 5, 8, 6, 8, 11

and *ab*

2, 6, 12, 5, 15, 30

I. The probability that $a + b$ is a prime number is $\dfrac{3}{6} = \dfrac{1}{2}$

II. The probability that $a + b > 8$ is $\dfrac{1}{6}$

III. The probability that $ab > a + b$ is $\dfrac{4}{6} = \dfrac{2}{3}$

As a result, only statement I is true, and the correct answer is A.

Solution 179: C

The cheetahs' population growth can be represented via a geometric sequence with initial number $= 4$ and rate 2:

Year 5: 4×2

Year 10: 4×2^2

Year 15: 4×2^3

Year 20: 4×2^4

Year 25: 4×2^5

The predicted difference between the cheetahs' population in year 25 versus year 15 is therefore $4(2^5 - 2^3) = 4(32 - 8) = 96$

Solution 180: B

For the expression in question to be undefined, the denominator has to be "0" or

$$x^2 + x - 6 = 0$$

To find the roots of the second degree equation, we can rewrite it as follows:

$$x^2 - 2x + 3x - 6 = x^2 + 3x - (2x + 6) =$$
$$x(x + 3) - 2(x + 3) =$$
$$(x + 3)(x - 2) = 0$$

which gives us the values of x for which the denominator of the equation is 0 or -3 and 2.

Solution 181: D

Short of plotting the function, the range can be calculating by identifying the largest and the smallest possible values for f.

The largest value is clearly obtained by substituting 7 for x, or
$$f(7) = 3 \times 7^2 - 5 = 3 \times 49 - 5 = 147 - 5 = 142$$

For the smallest value, one must observe that any negative value (including the smallest possible value for x, or -1) will still result in a positive value for $3x^2$. The same result applies to values of x between 0 and 1, or the contribution of $3x^2$ to the total value of the function is positive. As a result, the smallest contribution is when $x = 0$ and therefore $f(0) = -5$.

Solution 182: 28

Let the lengths of the third sides of the triangles T1 and T2 be $x1$ and $x2$, respectively. Given that the lengths of the other two sides are 15 and 25, one can define a range of values for the third sides as follows:
$$25 - 15 < x1 \text{ or } x2 < 25 + 15$$

or

$$10 < x1 < 40 \text{ and } 10 < x2 < 40$$
$$\text{MAX(PerT1} - \text{PerT2)} = \text{MAX}(x1 - x2) = \text{MAX}(x1) - \text{MIN}(x2) = 39 - 11 = 28$$

Solution 183: 1350

Let G and L be the greatest and the least integers in set A, respectively. Thus
$$G - L = 225$$

The difference between the "greatest" and the "least" integers in set B will be
$$(6G - 7) - (6L - 7) = 6(G - L) = 6 \times 225 = 1350$$

Solution 184: 8/21

The probability of satisfying condition (1) is

$$\frac{6}{5+4+6} \times \frac{5}{5+4+6-1} = \frac{6}{15} \times \frac{5}{14} = \frac{1}{7}$$

The probability of satisfying condition (2) is

$$\frac{5}{5+4+6} \times \frac{6}{5+4+6-1} + \frac{5}{5+4+6} \times \frac{4}{5+4+6-1} =$$

$$\frac{5}{15} \times \frac{6}{14} + \frac{5}{15} \times \frac{4}{14} =$$

$$\frac{1}{7} + \frac{2}{21} =$$

$$\frac{5}{21}$$

The probability of satisfying either condition (1) *or* condition (2) is therefore:

$$\frac{1}{7} + \frac{5}{21} = \frac{8}{21}$$

Note: Remember, "and" equals $\times$ (multiplication) and "or" equals $+$ (addition).

Solution 185: 5

In standard form, the equation of line *l*, $3x - 2y = 8$, becomes

$$y = \frac{3}{2}x - 4$$

Given that *l* and *n* are parallel, the slope of *l* must be equal to the slope of *n*, or $m = \frac{3}{2}$

In addition, line *n* passes through (–1, 2), so its equation ($y = mx + b$) can be written as

$$2 = -\frac{3}{2} + b \ \text{ or } \ b = \frac{7}{2}$$

It follows that $m + b = \frac{3}{2} + \frac{7}{2} = 5$

Solution 186: 27,000

Given that $15 = 3 \times 5$ and $20 = 2^2 \times 5$, the smallest integer divisible by 15 and 20 is

$$2^2 \times 3 \times 5 = 60$$

Given that N must be the cube of an integer (a), the smallest value for N that would also satisfy the divisibility conditions is

$$2^3 \times 3^3 \times 5^3 = [60 \times (2 \times 3^2 \times 5^2)] = 60 \times 450 = 27,000$$

Solution 187: 1500

If the original radius is R, the increased radius is $4R$. Considering the area of the circle with radius R as the reference, therefore representing 100%, by comparison, the area of the circle with radius $4R$ would be

$$\pi R^2 \ldots\ldots\ldots\ldots\ldots\ldots\ldots 100\%$$
$$\pi (4R)^2 \ldots\ldots\ldots\ldots\ldots\ldots x\%$$

or

$$x = 1600\%$$

As a result, the area of the circle increased by $1600\% - 100\% = 1500\%$

Solution 188: 35

Let the length of the third side be L. The perimeter of the triangle is therefore equal with $7 + 11 + L = 18 + L$.

The range of possible values for L is given by the following double inequality

$$11 - 7 < L < 11 + 7 \text{ or } 4 < L < 18$$

The greatest perimeter is obtained by maximizing the value of L, or considering the largest integer value for L that satisfies the above inequalities, or 17. Thus, the perimeter is

$$18 + 17 = 35$$

Solution 189: 76

The average score is equal to the sum of (1) scores obtained by the 20 students who were present at the test day plus (2) scores of the 5 students who made the test up at a later day divided by total number of students in the class, or 25.

Thus, the average score for the class was

$$\frac{20 \times 75 + 5 \times 80}{25} = \frac{1500 + 400}{25} = \frac{1900}{25} = 76$$

Chapter

Additional Problems

Example isn't another way to teach, it is the only way to teach.

—Albert Einstein

The answers to the problems in this chapter can be found in Chapter 11.

Problem 190

If
$0 \leq x \leq y$
and
$(x + y)^2 - (x - y)^2 \geq 36$

what is the smallest possible value of y?

Problem 191

Two printing presses, *M* and *N*, working together can complete a job in 4 hours. Working alone, press *M* can do the job in 20 hours. How many hours will press *N* take to do the job by itself?

Problem 192

How many sides does a polygon have if the measure of each interior angle is 5 times the degree measure of each exterior angle?

Problem 193

Five people shared a prize of $100. Each one received a whole number of dollars and no two people received the same amount.

If the largest share was $30 and the smallest one $15, what is the most money that the person with the third largest share could have received?

Problem 194

At time $t = 0$, a ball was thrown upward from an initial height of 10 ft. Until the ball hit the ground, its height (in feet) after t seconds was given by the function

$$h(t) = a - (b - 2t)^2,$$

where a and b are positive constants.

If the ball reached its maximum height of 110 ft at time $t = 5$ seconds, what was the height, in feet, of the ball at time $t = 2.5$ seconds?

Problem 195

In an amusement park, regulations require that a child be between 30" and 50" tall to ride a specific attraction. Which of the following inequalities can be used to determine whether or not a child's height h satisfies the regulation for this ride?

(A) $|h - 10| < 50$
(B) $|h - 20| < 40$
(C) $|h - 30| < 20$
(D) $|h - 40| < 10$

Problem 196

A jar contains 21 marbles: 6 red, 7 blue, and 8 green. If you remove one marble at a time, randomly, what is the minimum number that you must remove to be certain that you have at least 3 marbles of each color?

Problem 197

The number of victories per player of a tennis team is given in the following table:

# victories	# players
0	3
1	6
2	2
3	1

A new player joined the team and—as a result—the average number of victories per player became the median number of victories per player.

How many matches did the new player win?

Problem 198

If $N + 2$ is a multiple of 7, what is the remainder when N is divided by 7?

Problem 199

At a party, a catering company was paid to provide one sub sandwich for every 3 people, one bottle of soda for every 4 people, and one large ice cream cake for every 24 people. If the total number of subs, bottles of soda, and cakes was N, then—in terms of N—how many people were at the party?

Problem 200

In a survey of 50 people, 25 people subscribed to newspaper X, 35 people subscribed to newspaper Y, and 20 people subscribed to newspaper Z. For any two of the newspapers, 6 people subscribed to both newspapers but not the third one. If 2 people in the survey did not subscribe to any of the newspapers, how many people subscribed to all three newspapers?

Problem 201

If
2x − 3y = 6
3x − 2y + z = 9

then
x + y + z = ?

Problem 202

The average of three consecutive integers is N. Which of the following must be true?

I.   N is an integer.
II. One of the numbers is equal to N.
III. The average of two of the three numbers is N.

Problem 203

x	f(x)
0	m
1	40
2	n

If $f(x)$ is a linear function defined according to the table above, what is the value of $m + n$?

Problem 204

The distribution of grades on the final exam in math is shown below:

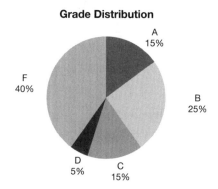

Grade Distribution

The total number of participating students is 1,000. What percent of the students who failed the exam would have had to pass it, in order for the percent of students passing the exam to be at least 90%?

Problem 205

X is the set of positive integers less than 18; Y is the set of positive integers that contain the digit 3; Z is the set of primes.

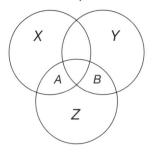

1. How many numbers are members of the region labeled A?
2. Which numbers less than 45 are members of the region labeled B?

Problem 206

Jason's lock combination consists of three, 2-digit numbers. Each set of numbers satisfies exactly one of the following conditions:

*   one number is odd
*   only one number is a multiple of 6
*   one number represents the day of the month Jason was born

Which of the following could be a combination to Jason's lock?

(A) 24-19-36
(B) 22-20-21
(C) 30-28-26
(D) 21-20-18

Problem 207

Two propositions were put forward for voting by a city council. Of the 33 city council members, 15 voted for proposition X, 25 voted for proposition Y, and 12 voted for both propositions. Which of the following statements must be true?

    I.   Ten members voted for proposition Y but not for proposition X.
    II. Five members voted against both propositions.
    III. Sixteen members voted for one proposition and against the other proposition.

(A) I only
(B) II only
(C) I & II only
(D) II & III only

Problem 208

If $\dfrac{2X}{3X} - 1 = -\dfrac{5}{17}$

What digit does X represent?

Problem 209

$$a \times 3^3 + b \times 3^2 + c \times 3 + d = 49$$

Each letter in the equation above represents a digit that is less than or equal to 2. What four-digit number does *abcd* represent?

Problem 210

A basketball team has 15 players. Each player shot 100 free throws, and the average number of baskets made was 80. If the lowest and the highest scores were eliminated, the average number of baskets for the remaining players was 82. What is the smallest number of baskets anyone on the team could have made?

Chapter 11

Solutions to Problems in Chapter 10

Anyone who has never made a mistake has never tried anything new.

—Albert Einstein

Solution 190: 3

We first need to write an equation expressing y as a function of x using the second inequality:

$$x^2 + 2xy + y^2 - x^2 + 2xy - y^2 \geq 36$$

or

$$4xy \geq 36$$

and thus

$$y \geq 9/x$$

Maximizing the value of y requires that we minimize (use the smallest possible value of) x. Given that $0 \leq x \leq y$, the smallest value of x happens to be y and we substitute that value in the expression of y to obtain

$$y \geq 9/y$$

or

$$y^2 \geq 9$$

Given that y is a positive number, this results in

$$y \geq 3$$

and thus the smallest value of *y* is 3.

Solution 191: 5

Observation #1: The number of hours a printing press is in action and its contribution (as in percentage of work done) to completing the job are directly proportional quantities (more hours, higher percentage of work done).

Observation #2: If more than one printing press is used, their work (percentage of job done) is cumulative.

With these in mind, we can set up the problem to outline the relationship (direct proportionality) among printing presses being used, the number of hours they operate, and the fraction of the task (job) completed during that time:

$M + N$ . . . . . . 4 [hours] . . . . 1 [complete the job]

and

M. . . . . 20 [hours] . . . . . . 1 [complete the job]

N. . . . . x [hours] . . . . 1 [complete the job]

Because these quantities are directly proportional, one can write

M. . . . . 1 [hour] . . . . $\dfrac{1}{20}$ [fraction of job completed]

N. . . . . 1 [hour] . . . . $\dfrac{1}{x}$ [fraction of job completed]

$M + N$ . . . . . . 1 [hour] . . . . $\dfrac{1}{20} + \dfrac{1}{x}$ [fraction of job completed]

$M + N$ . . . . . . 4 [hours] . . . . $4\left(\dfrac{1}{20} + \dfrac{1}{x}\right)$ [fraction of job completed]

Let's now compare the first and the last relationships shown above. The result is a first degree equation in *x*:

$$4\left(\frac{1}{20} + \frac{1}{x}\right) = 1$$

Note that all calculations have been postponed until the last step. It is now easy to see how simplifications can reduce calculations to a minimum, in this case to no calculations at all as simplifying the fraction should not require a calculator:

$$\frac{1}{5} + \frac{4}{x} = 1$$

or

$$\frac{4}{x} = \frac{4}{5}$$

or $x = 5$ [hours]

Solution 192: 12

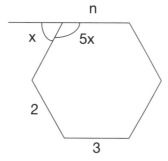

The fact that the ratio of each interior angle to its corresponding exterior one is constant (and equal to 5) indicates that *all* (interior) angles are equal, therefore the polygon is equilateral (regular).

First, we should calculate the measure of each interior angle of the polygon by noticing that

$$x + 5x = 6x = 180°$$
$$x = 30° \text{ (measure of exterior angle)}$$
$$5x = 150° \text{ (measure of interior angle)}$$

The total number of sides of the polygon (n) can then be obtained by writing an equation that gives us the sum of its interior angles using
1. the general formula derived in Problem 58, and
2. the calculated angle measure for its interior angles:

$$(n - 2) \times 180° = n \times 150°$$
$$n \times 180° - 360° = n \times 150°$$
$$n \times 30° = 360°$$
$$n = 12$$

Solution 193: 19

Let the numbers (in ascending order) be: 15, x, y, z, 30:

$$15 < x < y < z < 30$$

Their sum is 100. As a result

$$x + y + z = 100 - 15 - 30 = 55$$

The number representing the third largest share is y given by

$$y = 55 - (x + z)$$

To maximize the value of y, one has to minimize the value of $(x + z)$. The minimum value for x is 16. The minimum value for z is $y + 1$. We can now rewrite the equation above as

$$y = 55 - (16 + y + 1) = 38 - y$$
$$2y = 38$$
$$y = 19$$

Solution 194: 85

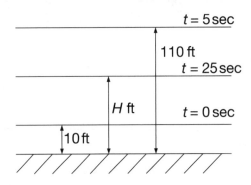

Let the value of the function at $t = 2.5$ sec be H:

$$h(2.5) = H$$

If we consider the motion equation (described above) at times 0, 2.5, and 5 seconds, respectively, we can write the following equations (with all heights being expressed in ft):

$$h(0) = 10 = a - b^2 \text{ (Equation 1)}$$
$$h(2.5) = H = a - (b - 5)^2 = a - b^2 + 10b - 25 \text{ (Equation 2)}$$
$$h(5) = 110 = a - (b - 10)^2 = a - b^2 + 20b - 100 \text{ (Equation 3)}$$

From equation 1, we substitute 10 for $a - b^2$ in Equation 3:

$$110 = 10 + 20b - 100 \text{ or } b = \frac{(110 + 100 - 10)}{20} = 10$$

Substituting the values for $a - b^2$ and b obtained above in Equation 2, one obtains:

$$H = 10 + 10 \times 10 - 25 = 10 + 100 - 25 = 85 \text{ [ft]}$$

Solution 195: D

By definition (see Section 3.28 on absolute value),

$$|h - a| = h - a; \text{ if } h > a$$
$$|h - a| = 0; \text{ if } h = a$$
$$|h - a| = -h + a; \text{ if } h < a$$

As a result, the general inequality $|h - a| < b$ can be written

$$h - a < b \text{ for } h > a \text{ or } a < h < a + b$$
$$-h + a < b \text{ for } h < a \text{ or } a - b < h < a$$

Combining the two inequalities above results in:

$$a - b < h < a + b$$

Because the problem states the condition $30 < h < 50$, it follows that

$$a - b = 30$$
$$a + b = 50$$

or

$$a = 40$$
$$b = 10$$

and therefore the solution is D.

Solution 196: 18

The keyword in the question is the word *certain*. In the context of this problem, it means that the result has to be 100% accurate under any circumstances and thus it implies that one has to assume the worst-case scenario. That leads us to an outcome where the first 15 marbles are not of the color of the marbles of which we have the least: red. Consequently, the first marbles removed are green (8) and blue (7). In addition and to satisfy the condition that the outcome contains at least 3 marbles of each color, we need to remove 3 red marbles for a total of 18 marbles.

Solution 197: 0

Let's first write in ascending order the 13 ($0 \times 3 + 1 \times 6 + 2 \times 2 + 3 \times 1$) numbers of victories for each one of the 12 ($3 + 6 + 2 + 1$) players:

$$0\ 0\ 0\ 1\ 1\ 1\ 1\ 1\ 1\ 2\ 2\ 3$$

It is easy to notice/calculate the median number of victories per player as being 1. Let's assume the number of victories of the new player is x. The average number of victories per player taking into account the new addition to the team is

$$AVE = \frac{\#\,victories}{\#\,players} = \frac{13 + x}{12 + 1} = \frac{13 + x}{13}$$

and this is equal to the median number of victories per player. It is now easy to assess that whether

$$x = 0$$
$$x = 1$$
$$x = 2$$
$$x = 3$$
$$x => 3$$

and we place anyone of these values in its corresponding position in the sequence of numbers (victories) in ascending order shown above, the median value of the sequence *will not change*, therefore it is still 1. As a result,

$$\frac{13 + x}{13} = 1$$

and therefore the total number of matches won by the new player (x) must be 0.

Solution 198: 5

Translating English to algebra, we write the equations that capture the information given in the text of the problem as follows:

$$N + 2 = 7 \times A \text{ or } N = 7 \times A - 2$$

and

$$N = 7 \times B + R$$

where A and B are integers, and R is the remainder of dividing N by 7 ($R < 7$).

Combining the two underlined equations above leads to

$$7 \times A - 2 = 7 \times B + R$$

or

$$R = 7 \times (A - B) - 2$$

If we interpret the equation above as "R is a multiple of 7 minus 2" and take into account that $R < 7$, the only acceptable value for R is

$$7 - 2 = 5$$

Solution 199: 8N/5

Let the numbers of subs, bottles of soda, and (ice cream) cakes be S, B, and C, respectively. According to the problem statement,

$$S + B + C = N \text{ (Equation 1)}$$

At the same time, with the notation introduced above and translating the information/data to algebra, one can write

$$3S = 4B = 24C = \text{number of people attending the party (Equation 2)}$$

One has to assume that everybody was treated equally, in other words, each person
   1. ate a sub, drank soda, and had a slice of cake, and
   2. at the end of the party there were no leftovers.

From the second equation, we have that

$$S = 8C \text{ and } B = 6C$$

We now substitute $8C$ and $6C$ for S and B in the first equation to obtain

$$8C + 6C + C = N$$
$$\text{or}$$
$$C = N/15$$

For the formula that gives us the total number of guests attending the party, we'll use "$24C$" and as a result,

$$\text{Total Number of People Attending the Party} = \frac{24N}{15} = \frac{8N}{5}$$

Solution 200: 7

To capture information relevant to solving this problem (i.e., all categories of subscribers), let's use the following notations:

X = number of people who subscribed to newspaper X and only X

Y = number of people who subscribed to newspaper Y and only Y

Z = number of people who subscribed to newspaper Z and only Z

XY = number of people who subscribed to newspapers X and Y

YZ = number of people who subscribed to newspapers Y and Z

ZX = number of people who subscribed to newspapers Z and X

XYZ = number of people who subscribed to all three newspapers

Note that in the above notations $XY \neq X \times Y, XYZ \neq X \times Y \times Z$, etc.

Solution #1 (using algebra only)

With the notations introduced above, using the translation of English to algebra technique, we obtain the following equations:

$$25 = X + XY + ZX + XYZ \quad \text{(Equation 1)}$$
$$35 = Y + XY + YZ + XYZ \quad \text{(Equation 2)}$$
$$20 = Z + ZX + YZ + XYZ \quad \text{(Equation 3)}$$

(for the number of people who subscribed to newspapers X, Y, and Z, respectively)

$$50 = X + Y + Z + XY + YZ + ZX + XYZ + 2 \quad \text{(Equation 4)}$$

(for the total number of people who participated in the survey)

Observation will play an important role in determining the next steps to work with the above equations. Inspecting the four equations above, for example, may suggest as a way to simplify the equations to simply add the Equations 1, 2, and 3 thus obtaining Equation 5:

$$80 = X + Y + Z + 2(XY + YZ + ZX) + 3XYZ \quad \text{(Equation 5)}$$

Now if you subtract Equation 4 from 5, you obtain Equation 6.

$$30 = XY + YZ + ZX + 2XYZ - 2 \quad \text{(Equation 6)}$$

The fact that "for any two of the newspapers, 6 people subscribed to both newspapers but not the third one" translates into Equation 7:

$$XY = YZ = ZX = 6 \text{ (Equation 7)}$$

Substituting Equation 7 in 6 gives us

$$30 = 6 + 6 + 6 + 2XYZ - 2$$

or

$$2XYZ = 14$$

or

$$XYZ = 7$$

Solution #2 (using Venn diagrams and algebra)

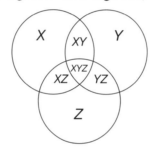

From the above Venn diagram—in which each oval represents the number of people who subscribed to newspapers X, Y, and Z, respectively—one can write the following equations:

$$25 = X + XY + ZX + XYZ$$
$$35 = Y + XY + YZ + XYZ$$
$$20 = Z + ZX + YZ + XYZ$$

(for the number of people who subscribed to newspapers X, Y, and Z, respectively) and

$$50 = X + Y + Z + XY + YZ + ZX + XYZ + 2$$

(for the total number of people who participated in the survey)

For the rest, we'll follow the same steps used in the first solution (add the first three equations to obtain):

$$80 = X + Y + Z + 2(XY + YZ + ZX) + 3XYZ$$

and subtracting the fourth equation from the result leading to

$$30 = XY + YZ + ZX + 2XYZ - 2$$

Substituting 6 for *XY*, *YZ*, and *ZX* in the above equation gives us the total number of subscribers to all three newspapers (*X*, *Y*, and *Z*) as being

$$XYZ = 7$$

Solution 201: 3

We should recall from algebra that to solve for three unknowns (i.e., *x*, *y*, and *z*), we need three (independent) equations. The fact that we only have two should discourage us from using a standard way of working with sets of equations (i.e., the substitution technique/approach) because we won't be able to solve for *x*, *y*, and *z*.

Based on this observation and given that we are asked to calculate the sum of the three unknowns, we conclude that it has to be done through a combination of the two given equations (multiplying each side by -1):

$$2x - 3y = 6$$
$$3x - 2y + z = 9$$

After taking note of the coefficients used in each equation, it's easy to observe that if we change signs in the first equation:

$$-2x + 3y = -6$$

and add it to the second equation, the latter becomes

$$3x - 2y + z - 2x + 3y = 9 - 6$$

or

$$x + y + z = 3$$

Solution 202: I, II, and III

Let the three consecutive integers be

$$X, X + 1, X + 2$$

The average of the three numbers is

$$\frac{X + X + 1 + X + 2}{3} = \frac{3X + 3}{3} = X + 1 = N$$

X + 1 is an integer and so is *N*. Consequently Statement I is true.

$N = X + 1$, which is one of the consecutive integers (the middle one) and as such, Statement II is also true.

The average of the first and the third integers (X and $X + 2$) is the middle integer ($X + 1$). As a result, Statement III is true too.

In conclusion, Statements I, II, and III are all true.

Solution 203: 80

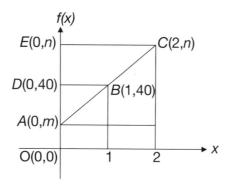

The table in Problem 203 is illustrated in the figure above where $f(x)$ is represented in the xy coordinate system.

This representation shows the symmetry of the problem and allows us to observe a simple way to convert the information given to us into equations. Triangles $\triangle ABD$ and $\triangle ACE$ are similar.

As a result, the following relationship between their sides can be written:

$$\frac{AD}{AE} = \frac{DB}{EC}$$

or

$$\frac{40 - m}{n - m} = \frac{1}{2}$$

$$80 - 2m = n - m$$

and the result is:

$$n + m = 80$$

Solution 204: 75

Let the population of students who passed and failed the test be P and F, respectively. The percentages of students who passed and failed were
$$A + B + C + D = 15\% + 25\% + 15\% + 5\% = 60\%$$
$$100\% - P = 40\%$$

thus

$$P = 60\% \text{ of } 1000 = 0.6 \times 1000 = 600$$
$$F = 40\% \text{ of } 1000 = 0.4 \times 1000 = 400$$

Because the objective is to increase the percentage of passing students from 60% to 90% (i.e., the number of passing students would increase from 600 to 900), it follows that 300 students out of the 400 students who initially failed the test would have to pass. We can set this up as follows:
$$400. . . . . .100\%$$
$$300. . . . . .x\%$$

Cross multiplication leads to $x = 30,000/400\% = 75\%$, therefore 75% of the students who initially failed would have to subsequently pass in order for the passing student population to increase from 60% to 90%.

Solution 205: 5 and 4

Based on the definitions given in the text of the problem, the sets of numbers in question are:
$$X: 1, 2, 3, 4, . . . , 16, 17$$
$$Y: 3, 13, 23, 30, 31, 32, 33, . . . , 39, 43, 53, . . .$$
$$Z: 2, 3, 5, 7, 11, 13, 17, 19, . . .$$

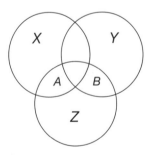

Note that the numbers of region A are numbers that belong to the intersection of regions X and Z from which we need to subtract what regions X, Y, and *Z* have in common—the intersection of *X*, *Y*, and *Z*. Consequently, the numbers that belong to region *A* are:

$$\{2, 3, 5, 7, 11, 13, 17\} - \{3, 13\} = \{2, 5, 7, 11, 17\}$$

to find that region *A* has 5 numbers.

Moving now to region *B*, its content is made up of numbers less than 45 that represent the intersection of sets *Y* and *Z* from which we need to subtract the intersection of all sets—*X*, *Y*, and *Z*. As a result, region *B* includes the following set of numbers:

$$\{3, 13, 23, 31, 37, 43\} - \{3, 13\} = \{23, 31, 37, 43\}$$

Therefore, region *B* has four numbers.

Solution 206: D

Note the keyword "exactly"—meaning that when we look at the options A through D, no number should satisfy more than one of the three conditions.

With this in mind,

  We eliminate A because two numbers are multiples of 6 (24 and 36).
  We eliminate B because none of the three numbers is a multiple of 6.
  We eliminate C because none of the three numbers is odd.

We choose D because only one number is a multiple of 6 (18) and one is odd (21), with the third one (20) being neither and therefore could be assumed to be Jason's day of birth.
  The result is therefore D.

Solution 207: D

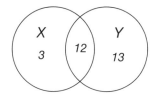

The above Venn diagram captures the information given in the text of the problem.

As exemplified in Problems 200 and 205, one way to approach this problem is by identifying all categories of players:

- council members who voted for X and against Y (15 −12 = 3),
- council members who voted for Y and against X (25 − 12 = 13), and
- council members who voted for both X and Y (12).

The remaining number,

$$33 - 3 - 13 - 12 = 5$$

represents a final category of council members, the one identified in the problem as "members who voted against both propositions."

As a result, we already validated that Condition II is true.

Condition I is false as, according to the Venn diagram, 13 (not 10) council members voted for Y and against X.

Condition III is true as the number of council members who voted for one proposition and against the other is equal to the members who voted for X and against Y (3) plus the members who voted for Y and against X (13): 16.

The correct answer is D.

Solution 208: 4

Note that X is a "digit" (i.e., an integer equal to 0, 1, 2, . . . , or 9) and consequently

$$5X \neq 5 \times X$$

The correct representation of unknown digits is done via representation of Base 10 numbers (numbers in the Base 10 numeral system). For example, when using Base 10, you would write

$$1952 \text{ as } 1 \times 10^3 + 9 \times 10^2 + 5 \times 10^1 + 2$$

and

$$8A5B3 \text{ as } 8 \times 10^4 + A \times 10^3 + 5 \times 10^2 + B \times 10^1 + 3$$

By the same token,

$$2X = 20 + X \text{ and } 3X = 30 + X$$

and, as a result, the initial equation can be rewritten as

$$\frac{2X}{3X} = \frac{20 + X}{30 + X} = 1 - \frac{5}{17} = \frac{12}{17}$$

$$340 + 17 \times X = 360 + 12 \times X$$

$$5 \times X = 20$$

$$X = 4$$

Solution 209: 1211

One way to solve this problem is by combining trial and error and observation. Let's just start by noticing that each digit (a, b, c, or d) can take on only one of the following values: 0, 1, 2. In addition, it will help if we rewrite the equation as:

$$27 \times a + 9 \times b + 3 \times c + d = 49$$

Observation #1: a cannot be 2 ($27 \times 2 = 54 > 49$) or 0 (even if we used maximum values for b, c, and d, the sum of the remaining terms will still be less than 49). As a result, $a = 1$, and the equation gets simplified to

$$9 \times b + 3 \times c + d = 49 - 27 = 22$$

Observation #2: b cannot be 1 as assigning maximum values to the remaining digits will still not add up to 22. Consequently $b = 2$ and the equation gets further simplified to

$$3 \times c + d = 22 - 9 \times 2 = 4$$

Observation #3: c cannot be 0 or 2 as this would result in $d = 4$ (whereas d can only be 0, 1, or 2) or $d < 0$. Thus, $c = 1$ and therefore $d = 4 - 3 = 1$.

The four digit number (abcd) that satisfied the given equation is therefore

1211

Solution 210: 34

Let's consider the number of baskets made by the worst and the best performers on the team as being L and H, respectively, and the total number of baskets made by each player on the team except the worst and the best performers as being X. With this notation and translating the text of the problems to algebra, we obtain the following equations:

$$L + X + H = 15 \times 80 = 1200$$

$$X = 13 \times 82 = 1066$$

Substituting 1066 for X in the first equation gives us
$$L + H = 1200 - 1066 = 134$$

To minimize L—as to obtain the "smallest number of baskets anyone could have made"—we have to maximize H, and given that the maximum value for H is 100, it follows that
$$L = 134 - H = 134 - 100 = 34$$

Chapter

Test Analysis

Not all who wander are lost.

—J. R. R. Tolkien

Sample Test

Using the online sample test provided, you can and should be able to assess where you are in your preparation for the SAT. Page 269 includes a sample of the printout available to you upon completion of the test. Please note that to correspond with the actual SAT (which provides the verbal portion first as Sections 1 and 2), the sections of the sample math test have been labeled as Section 3 and Section 4. Also note that the final printout may appear slightly different in design from this sample and will include the student's answers in comparison to the correct answers.

Using the Online Test

After you becomes familiar with the content of the book, I recommend that you take the sample test. To administer a test and received a thorough analysis of the result, take the following steps:

1. Go to http://www.prufrock.com/perfect800.
2. Follow the instructions on the screen. You may want to have scrap paper available for working problems.
3. When completed, be sure to print a copy of the analysis of your results.

To access the online test, please visit:
http://www.prufrock.com/perfect800

SAT (Math): Analysis of Results
Sample Test

Student Data

Last Name	First Name	Date	Total Score (Goal)	Heart of Algebra (Goal)	Problem Solving and Data Analysis (Goal)	Passport to Advanced Math (Goal)
Doe	J.	07/31/16	780	14	14	14

	Total	Heart of Algebra	Problem Solving and Data Analysis	Passport to Advanced Math
Raw Score	53	18	15	15
SAT Score/Subscore	740	15	13	14
Actual Score vs. Goal [%]	94.87	107.14	92.86	100.00
ACT Score (equivalent)	31			

General Findings

Skills	%	Qualifier	Rationale
Overall Knowledge	91.38	Good	It is assumed that the overall knowledge is directly proportional with (is measured by the) overall performance.
Critical Thinking/ Analytic Skills	88.95	Satisfactory	It is assumed that the critical thinking/analytic skills can be estimated—in general—by one's ability to solve problems that are not straightforward applications of memorized formulas/techniques, require identification of information that is relevant to answering the question/solving the problem, and a translation of English into a "math language" (like Algebra). The student's ability to correctly solve open-ended problems and answer questions with a level of difficulty above average is also taken into account.
Concentration/ Focus	103.13	Excellent	For the purpose of this analysis, concentration/focus is a measure of a student's ability to maintain a constant concentration level for a period of time equal to the test duration. It is assumed that that concentration/focus can be estimated by analyzing factors such as the number of "silly mistakes" (e.g., incorrect answers to "easy" problems), the ability to answer questions in a timely manner (e.g., number of problems the students couldn't solve because they ran out of time, eventually forcing them to answer with wild guesses), and the students' performance in solving word problems that require a fair amount of reading comprehension skills.
Reading Comprehension	89.80	Good	Critical reading skills are essential for academic achievement in any test/topic/discipline. It is assumed that reading comprehension skills—as required in the math sections of the test—can be estimated by looking at the student's performance in solving mostly word and open-ended problems that require a good understanding of the information available in the text of the problem and the ability to extract what's relevant to be used in the reasoning that leads to the required solution.

Qualifiers

94	<	Score (%)			Excellent
89	<	Score (%)	≤	94	Good
79	<	Score (%)	≤	89	Satisfactory
59	<	Score (%)	≤	79	Needs Improvement
		Score (%)	≤	59	Weak

Student's Math Academic "Holes"

Item Type	%	Qualifier
Multiple-Choice	91.11	Good
Open-Ended	92.31	Good
Content-Specific Skills	**%**	**Qualifier**
Arithmetic	100.00	Excellent
Algebra	92.11	Good
Miscellanoeus	88.89	Satisfactory
Subscore Topics	**%**	**Qualifier**
Heart of Algebra	94.74	Excellent
Problem Solving and Data Analysis	88.24	Satisfactory
Passport to Advanced Math	93.75	Good

Recommendations

Areas/Skills	Qualifier	What to do?
Knowledge	Good	Keep up with the good work. Challenge yourself by concentrating on the few areas identified in "Specific Findings" as areas where you need to improve. Review Sections 2.1 ("Factual Knowledge") and 2.2 ("The Identification of Weaknesses Approach") in the book.
Critical Thinking	Satisfactory	You need to improve your analytic skills, assuming that being "average" is not enough for you. Concentrate on solving "word" and "open-ended" problems, in particular those rated "hard" that require a "multistep" approach and translation of English into a "math language" (e.g., algebra.) In addition, you should try to improve your reading comprehension/critical reading skills. Review Sections 2.1 ("Analytic/Critical Thinking Skills"), 2.2 ("The Take-the-Challenge Approach"), 2.3, 2.4, 2.5, and 2.7 in the book.
Concentration	Excellent	Congratulations—Your ability to concentrate and focus on problem solving, for the entire duration of the test, was excellent! Keep on doing what you're doing!

Difficulty Levels
- Easy
- Medium
- Hard

Raw Score	Score	Raw Score	Heart of Algebra	Problem Solving and Data Analysis	Passport to Advanced Math
0	200	0	1	1	1
1	200	1	1	2	2
2	210	2	2	3	3
3	230	3	3	4	5
4	250	4	5	5	6
5	270	5	6	6	7
6	290	6	6	7	8
7	300	7	7	8	9
8	320	8	8	8	9
9	330	9	9	9	10
10	340	10	9	10	11
11	360	11	10	10	11
12	370	12	11	11	12
13	380	13	11	12	13
14	390	14	12	13	13
15	410	15	13	13	14
16	420	16	13	14	15
17	430	17	14	15	
18	440	18	15		
19	450	19	15		
20	460				
21	470				
22	480				
23	490				
24	500				
25	510				
26	530				
27	540				
28	550				
29	560				
30	570				
31	580				

Raw Score	Score	Raw Score	Heart of Algebra	Problem Solving and Data Analysis	Passport to Advanced Math
32	580				
33	590				
34	600				
35	610				
36	620				
37	630				
38	630				
39	640				
40	650				
41	660				
42	660				
43	670				
44	680				
45	680				
46	690				
47	690				
48	700				
49	710				
50	710				
51	720				
52	730				
53	740				
54	750				
55	770				
56	780				
57	790				
58	800				

Chapter 13

Mind Games

I have no special talents. I am only passionately curious.

—Albert Einstein

A number of mind/logic games are described on the following pages. Use them to sharpen your analytic skills. Mind/logic games often include information that is irrelevant to finding the correct answer. This is a way to add a magic flavor to them, for fun, but many times this information is also used to disguise an effort to lead you on a path to nowhere, thus testing your problem-solving stamina. Solutions are found in Chapter 14.

Mind Game 1

A hunter leaves his tent and walks 3.14 miles south and then 3.14 miles east and finally sees a bear. He shoots and kills it and then drags it for 3.14 miles going north, which brought him back to his tent. What color is the bear?

Mind Game 2

A chemical analysis of a tomato results in the discovery that most of it (i.e., its primary ingredient) is water. Analysis of a quantity of fresh tomato purchased by a distributor found 99% water and 1% "tomato" (the sum of all solid ingredients or everything that was not water). The tomatoes were stored (or left to dry out) in a warehouse. After a while, the businessman decided to sell the tomatoes to another distributor, rather than directly to a retailer. Local regulations dictated that the analysis be repeated, and the result of it indicated that the whole quantity lost 1% of its water content (i.e., the water content was reduced to 98%). Explain what happened and quantify the impact of this process on the total weight of the tomatoes purchased by the second distributor.

Mind Game 3

A magician has three cards: two with a picture of a goat and one with a picture of a car. He shuffles the cards and puts them face down on a table. The goal is for you to get the card showing the car. He asks you to select one card. Before you lift it up, the magician picks one of the other two and shows it to you. This card shows the picture of a goat. Then he asks you if you want to think again and decide whether you should pick the other remaining card instead. What should you do and why? (This is a version of the Monty Hall Problem also featured in the movie *21*.)

Mind Game 4

In a village, in a remote country, the elders got together and decided that all of the men living in the village should shave their beards. They also decided that everyone—without exception—should be given two options: either to do it themselves or go to the only barber in the village. All of the men in the village agreed that this was fair. Who shaves the barber?

Mind Game 5

A company is using an old building for its headquarters. Located on a large property, the building is also housing an indoor garage for the parking needs of the employees.

The company decided to go ahead with a construction project for a major makeover with the objective to shorten the commute of all employees. A contest for the best plan to achieve this objective is underway. Submit your own plan!

Mind Game 6

A homeless man collects 43 empty soda cans. A local convenient store redeems them for cash but only in batches of 7, for which it pays 35 cents. After the homeless man redeemed his cans according to the store policy, the owner presents him with a gift: a six-pack of the same soda. How much money can the homeless man make after he gets rid of all his cans?

Mind Game 7

Two trains are running toward each other on the same track, each one's speed being 10 miles/hour. Thus, they are heading toward a head-on collision. Initially, the distance between them is 10 miles. A mosquito is flying between them at constant speed equal to 20 miles/hour. What distance will the mosquito have covered at the time it is squashed by the two train engines?

Mind Game 8

Three players sit around a table wearing hats that display a positive number. The players know that one number is equal to the sum of the other two. After having time to familiarize themselves with the other players' numbers, the participants are asked to guess the number written on the hat they are wearing. A dialogue starts with one player saying: "I can't figure out my number." A second player says: "My number is 21." What are the three numbers in question?

Mind Game 9

A pedestrian runs into two people at the point where the road forks and does not know which way to go to get to his final destination. He knows that the two people are a liar and a truth-teller but does not know who is who. He can only ask one of them one question. What does he have to ask to be certain that the answer will point him in the right direction?

Mind Game 10

Four explorers arrive at a narrow bridge in the middle of the night. They can cross it in 1, 3, 5, and 10 minutes. A maximum of two of them can cross the bridge at the same time and the darkness prevents them from crossing the bridge without a flashlight. If more than one explorer were to cross the bridge, the calculated crossing time is equal to the time needed by the slowest of them. It's been a rough journey and they're down to one flashlight that still works. Devise a scenario the team must follow to cross the bridge in no more than 20 minutes.

Mind Game 11

How does one measure *exactly* 4 gallons with one 3-gallon bucket and one 5-gallon bucket?

Mind Game 12

A cruise ship is anchored in the San Francisco Bay. A 30-foot rope ladder is hanging on a side of the liner, reaching down to the water level. It is high-tide time and the ocean level is rising at a rate of 6 feet per hour. If this trend were to continue indefinitely, in how many hours will the tide overflow the ship?

Mind Game 13

The guards asked three prisoners to line up in the prison's backyard. The inmates were under strict instructions to stand still, look ahead, and wait for the guards' commands.

A guard picked up three hats from a basket that had 2 black and 3 white hats, and was located behind the last prisoner. Coming from behind, the guard would place a hat on each prisoner's head such that the inmates could only see the color of the hat worn by prisoners ahead of them in line, if any.

Next, the guards ordered the inmates, starting with the last, all the way to the first in line, to say if they could tell with 100% certainty the color of the hat they're wearing.

The last prisoner says: "I can't tell!" The next in line says: "I can't tell either!" Finally, the first prisoner says: "Yes, I do know the color of my hat!" What color was the hat worn by the first inmate?

Mind Game 14

A blindfolded magician hands a randomly selected spectator a deck of 52, all facedown, unmarked cards. The spectator is asked to pick any number of cards, count them while turning them over (face up), mix them up with the remaining cards, and shuffle the deck. After complying with this request, the spectator tells the magician how many cards were turned over. He or she then returns the deck of cards to the magician who—still blindfolded—separates the cards—behind his back—into two decks and returns them to the spectator who will find that the two decks contained an *equal number of cards* facing up.

Explain the trick!

Mind Game 15

A supermarket received three crates with veggies from a farm. Each crate contained regular potatoes, sweet potatoes, or a mix of the two potato varieties. The supermarket manager is informed that, although the labels were printed correctly, a junior-level employee at the warehouse labeled all of the crates incorrectly.

The manager is allowed to pick only one vegetable from any crate without looking inside the respective crate. Knowing what he or she ended up picking, the manager was subsequently able to correctly relabel the crates. How was this done?

Mind Game 16

From the very bottom of a 55-foot well, a worm started to crawl up toward the top. During the day, it advances 5 feet, but at night, it slides down 3 feet. How many days will the worm need to reach the top of the well?

Mind Game 17

The faces of a couple of dice are to be marked with numbers according to the following rules:

- the numbers to be used could be 0 or positive integers
- multiple use of the same number—if needed—is allowed only on one die
- the probability that the sum of the numbers representing the outcome of rolling the dice be 1, 2, 3, 4, 5, 6, 7, 8, 9, 10, 11, or 12 must be the same.

Find at least one combination of numbers to satisfy the above requirements.

Mind Game 18

A magician has two strings, each one of which, if set on fire from one end, would completely burn in 20 minutes. Without using a clock/watch and given a box of matches to light up the strings, the magician challenged the audience to find a way to measure out *exactly* 15 minutes. How can it be done?

Mind Game 19

Four classmates, Mary, John, Anna, and Eric, challenged each other to a race. The judge, Avery, was not present but accepted the task of awarding the participants certificates based on their performance. To do so, Avery wanted to meet each student privately, but Eric had to stay home with flu-like symptoms and only the other three students were available for an interview.

Being asked who came in first, second, and third, respectively, Eric's classmates responded as follows: Mary said "Anna, John, Eric," John said "Mary, Anna, Eric," and Anna responded "Eric, Mary, John."

Avery knows that *only one* of the statements made by her classmates was true. What's shown on the awards for each of the four students who participated in the race?

Mind Game 20

Of the 60 tokens stored in a box, 30 are white and 30 are black. After having removed 6 white and 7 black, Jeremy will take an additional 17 tokens from the box to engage in a token exchange with one of his friends. What is the least number of these additional tokens that must be white in order for Jeremy to have more white than black tokens to show to his friend?

Mind Game 21

Adam and Tom just met Maria. "When is your birthday?" Adam asked Maria. Maria thought a second and said,

"I'm not going to tell you, but I'll give you some clues." She wrote down a list of 10 dates:

> » May 15, May 16, May 19, June 17, June 18, July 14, July 16, August 14, August 15, August 17

"My birthday is one of these," she said.

Then, Maria whispered in Adam's ear the month and in Tom's the day of her birthday.

"Can you figure it out?" she asked her new friends.

Adam said, "I don't know when your birthday is, but I know Tom doesn't know either."

Tom replied, "I didn't know originally, but now I do."

Adam then said, "Well, now I know too!"

When is Maria's birthday?

On Your Own Problem 23

If John is a member of the local swim and tennis club, indicate from which of the following statements it can be determined whether or not John is a member of the local golf club.

    (A) Some people who are not in the swim and tennis club are not in the golf club

    (B) Anyone who is not in the swim and tennis club is not in the golf club

    (C) No one is in both the swim and tennis club and the golf club

    (D) Not everybody in the swim and tennis club is in the golf club

On Your Own Problem 24

On the playgrounds of a nursery school, there is a box containing building blocks of different colors and shapes. If some of the cubes are red, which of the following statements must be true?

    I.   If a block is red, then it is a cube.

    II.   If a block is not a cube, then it is not red.

    III.   If a block is not red, then it may be a cube.

    (A) I only

    (B) I and III only

    (C) III only

    (D) II only

On Your Own Problem 25

A jar contains 15 green and 15 yellow marbles. Calculate the least number of marbles that would have to be removed from the jar such that the ratio of green to yellow marbles left in the jar will be 3 to 2.

Chapter 14

Solutions to Mind Games

Failure is the condiment that gives success its flavor.

—Truman Capote

I have not failed. I've just found 10,000 ways that won't work.

—Thomas Edison

Mind Game Solution 1

The apparent paradox in this problem (how can one walk the same distance going south, then east, and then north and arrive at the point of departure?) has to do with our tendency to think two-dimensionally.

Rather than being flat, the Earth, as a three-dimensional object, is a sphere. Any location on Earth is described by two numbers—its latitude and its longitude.

Any movement on our planet can be described as a movement along lines of latitude (going EAST-WEST) and longitude (going NORTH-SOUTH). Lines of latitude are circles of different size. The longest is the Equator, whose latitude is zero, while at the poles—at latitudes 90° North and 90° South (or −90°)—the circles shrink to a point. As a result, the only location on Earth from which walking the same distance first South, then East and finally North will bring us back to the point of departure is the North Pole. Thus, the hunter killed a polar bear and the answer is white.

Note: The 3.14 mile distance was obviously a way to break your concentration, throw you on the wrong path, and take advantage of your tendency to occasionally overanalyze (e.g., make a connection to π and thus reach a dead end).

Mind Game Solution 2

Let A be the weight of the initial quantity of tomatoes. We are told that

Water = 99% of A or $0.99A$ which means that

"Tomato" = 1% of A or $0.01A$

The quantity of tomatoes was stored for a while during which time some of the water in its content evaporated. As a result, when the test was repeated, because water was lost, the total weight decreased to a value B where $B < A$.

The result of the new analysis concluded that

Water = 98% of B or $0.98B$ and

"Tomato" = 2% of B or $0.02B$

Given that the solid content of the tomatoes (which we referred to as "tomatoes") has not changed, it follows that

$$0.02 \times B = 0.01 \times A$$

or

$$B = \frac{A}{2}$$

This means that a 1% loss in water has resulted in 50% decrease in the weight of the tomatoes, and the second buyer had to pay for half the quantity that the first buyer paid for!

Mind Game Solution 3

One way to think about this problem is to consider the sample space (the set of all possible outcomes in probability theory) that the magician alters by turning over a card showing a goat. In doing so, he effectively removes one of the two losing cards from the sample space.

We will assume that there is a winning card—C—and that the two remaining ones, *A* and *B*, both have pictures showing goats. You are the contestant. There are three options:

- You first choose the card (*C*) showing a car. The magician then shows you either cards *A* or *B*, which reveals a goat. If you change your choice of cards (i.e., picking *A* or *B* instead of *C* which you originally picked), you lose. If you stay with your original choice, you win.
- Your first pick is card *A*. The magician then shows you card *B*, which displays a goat. If you switch to the remaining card, you win by getting the car; otherwise, you lose.
- You first choose card *B*. The magician then shows you card *A*, which displays a goat. If you switch to the remaining card (*C*), you win by getting the car; otherwise, you lose.

Each of the above three options has a ⅓ probability of occurring, because you are equally likely to begin by choosing any one of the three cards. In two of the above options, you win the car if you switch cards; in only one of the options you end up winning if you do not switch cards. When you switch, you win the car twice (the number of favorable outcomes) out of three possible options (the sample space). Thus, the probability of winning the car is ⅔ if you switch cards, which means that you should always switch cards (i.e., go for the second option when a card showing a goat was removed from the game).

This result (⅔) may seem counterintuitive because we may believe that the probability of winning the car should be ½ once the magician has shown that card *A* or *B* does not display the car. Many people reason that because there are two cards left, only one of which showing the car, the probability of winning must be ½. This would mean that switching cards would not make a difference. As we've shown above through the three different options, however, this is not the case.

Mind Game Solution 4

The barber cannot be the correct answer because it does not meet the requirement that "every man should be given two options" unless . . . the barber is a woman!

Mind Game Solution 5

Assumption #1: One-story building

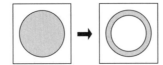

Solution:

Note the gray area (i.e., office space) in the original and in the proposed design. No matter how scattered the employees' homes outside the company premises (the square) were, each one's commute (defined as an idealized straight line connecting their homes with their office location) is shortened.

Assumption #2: Multistory building

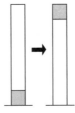

Solution:

Note the gray area designating the position of the indoor garage in the original building and in the proposed one. No matter how scattered the employees' homes outside the company premises were, each one's commute (defined as an idealized straight line connecting their homes with their office location) is shortened.

Mind Game Solution 6

After his find, the homeless man can bring to the store 6 complete sets of 7 empty cans and he's still left with one. After he finishes drinking the ones he received as a gift, he can add 6 cans to the one left from the original transaction and can now redeem one more complete set of cans. In total, he will have redeemed 7 sets and collected 7×35 cents = $2.45.

Mind Game Solution 7

We can calculate the total time until collision as being equal to

$$\frac{\text{DISTANCE}}{\text{RATE}} = \frac{10[\text{mi}]}{(10[\text{mi}\,/\,\text{h}] + 10[\text{mi}\,/\,\text{h}])} = 0.5[\text{h}] = 30[\text{min}]$$

In 30 minutes, the mosquito, flying at 20 mph, would have covered:

$$0.5\,[\text{h}] \times 20\,[\text{mph}] = 10\,[\text{miles}].$$

Mind Game Solution 8

Let the first player, the second player to speak, and the silent one be players 1, 2, and 3, respectively. The path to the correct answer starts with the observation that each player is normally contemplating two solutions:
- their number is either the sum of the two numbers, or
- their number is the difference between the largest and the smallest numbers seen on the other two players' hats.

As a result, they cannot predict with 100% accuracy their own number.

Following that, one should ask oneself under what circumstances the player who talks first—Player 1—would not have to choose between the two equally acceptable options described above. The answer is that only a player who sees two equal numbers would be in that position. In that case, he or she would know that his or her number is twice the number seen on the other players' hats. ("0" is not an acceptable solution as the problem states that the number must be positive.)

Continuing this line of reasoning, one should ask next under what circumstances the second speaker—Player 2—would be in a position to know with 100% accuracy his or her number.

The correct answer must eliminate one of the two equally valid options described earlier, capitalizing on the previous observation (i.e., excluding the possibility of Player 1 seeing two identical numbers). In the only valid scenario, Player 2 must see that the numbers of Players 1 and 3 are in the 2-to-1 ratio, respectively.

Let the numbers for Players 1 and 3 be $2x$ and x. In that case, Player 2's number can theoretically be (a) $3x = (2x + x)$ or (b) $x = (2x - x)$. The second option is eliminated because it implies that Players 2 and 3 have the same numbers and in that case, Player 1 would have been able to guess his or her number with 100% certainty. This is illustrated in the diagram below.

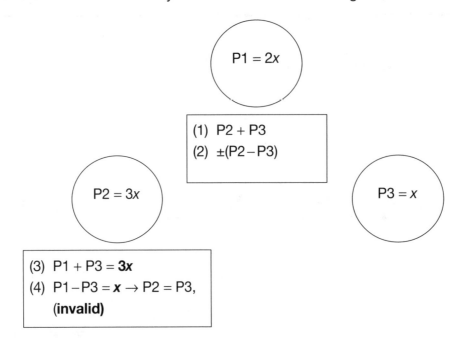

In conclusion, the numbers worn by Players 3, 1, and 2 are in that ratio 1:2:3, respectively, where Player 2's number is $21 = 3x$. x is 7 and thus the numbers for Players 1 and 3 are 14 ($2x$) and 7 (x).

Mind Game Solution 9

The pedestrian is only allowed one question and the person to whom he will address this question could be either a liar or a truth-teller. These restrictions should lead us to formulating a question on the opinion of the pedestrian that we chose not to talk to. For example, "If I asked your friend—standing next to you here—which way I should go to reach my final destination, what answer would I get?"

Option #1: The pedestrian is talking to the liar. In this case, the answer he or she will get must be a lie and the pedestrian will have to pick the other road.

Option #2: The pedestrian is talking to the truth-teller. In this case, the answer he will get is a true rendition of what the liar would say and the pedestrian, again, will have to pick the other road.

In conclusion, the question above is correct and to get to his final destination the pedestrian will have to chose the road opposite to the one recommended by the person questioned.

Mind Game Solution 10

The need to minimize the crossing time requires that the bridge be crossed by groups of two explorers with one returning to bring the flashlight (remember that there's only one that still works) to the next group.

In devising a workable scenario, one needs to

(1) minimize the time spent returning the flashlight (meaning that, if possible, the fastest explorers would be in charge of that task), and

(2) group the slowest explorers together and ensure that none of them will be sent back with the flashlight (see also 1).

Let's identify the explorers as 1, 3, 5, and 10. The above observations lead to a scenario shown in the table below:

	Explorers		Elapsed crossing
waiting to cross the bridge	crossing the bridge	having crossed the bridge	time / total time (minutes)
5, 10	>> 1 and 3 >>	1, 3	3 / 3
5, 10	<< 1 <<	3	1 / 4
1	>> 5 and 10 >>	3, 5, 10	10 / 14
1	<< 3 <<	5, 10	3 / 17
–	>> 1 and 3 >>	1, 3, 5, 10	3 / 20

Mind Game Solution 11

The following tables show two solutions to the problem, starting with the two buckets (3- and 5-gallons) being empty:

Step #	Action	Quantity of Water in the 3-Gal. Bucket	Quantity of Water in the 5-Gal. Bucket
0	Initial state	0	0
1	Fill up the 3-gal.	3	0
2	Empty the 3-gal. into the 5-gal.	0	3
3	Fill up the 3-gal.	3	3
4	Fill up the 5-gal. with water from the 3-gal.	1	5
5	Empty the 5-gal.	1	0

Step #	Action	Quantity of Water in the 3-Gal. Bucket	Quantity of Water in the 5-Gal. Bucket
6	Pour what's left in the 3-gal. into the 5-gal.	0	1
7	Fill up the 3-gal.	3	1
8	Empty the 3-gal. into the 5-gal.	0	**4**

or (even better, 6 steps instead of 8 steps)

Step #	Action	Quantity of Water in the 3-Gal. Bucket	Quantity of Water in the 5-Gal. Bucket
0	Initial state	0	0
1	Fill up the 5-gal.	0	5
2	Fill up the 3-gal. from the 5-gal.	3	2
3	Empty the 3-gal.	0	2
4	Empty the 5-gal. into the 3-gal.	2	0
5	Fill up the 5-gal.	2	5
6	Fill up the 3-gal. from the 5-gal.	3	**4**

Mind Game Solution 12

Never! (The ship . . . floats.)

Mind Game Solution 13

The following table shows—exhaustively—the possible color arrangements of the prisoners' hats:

Option #	Prisoner First in Line	Prisoner Second in Line	Prisoner Third (Last) in Line
1	W	W	W/B
2	B	B	W
3	W	B	W/B
4	B	W	W/B

The last prisoner spoke first and, because he could not tell the color of his hat, we conclude that option #2 is out.

The prisoner in the middle spoke next and with option #2 out and given his answer, we conclude that option #4 is also out, because if he saw that the first prisoner's hat was black, his options were limited to only one (option #4) as he would be certain that his hat was white.

In conclusion, the first prisoner was wearing a **white** hat, as the only options left were 1 and 3.

Mind Game Solution 14

Assume the spectator turned over N cards, which subsequently were mixed up with the remaining cards, and returned the deck to the magician. The latter, behind his back, would separate the cards into two decks, the first one consisting of N cards. If x cards in the first deck were turned up, the number of cards facing up in the second deck would be $N-x$. As a result, all the magician has to do is turn over each card in the first deck (resulting in the number of cards facing up being $N-x$) and return it, together with the unchanged second deck to the spectator. The spectator would then have two decks of cards, each one containing **$N - x$** cards facing up.

Mind Game Solution 15

Assume the following notations for the content of the crates: p, sp, and $p\&sp$ as abbreviations for potatoes, sweet potatoes, and both kinds of potatoes, respectively. The following table shows all possible options for the content of the incorrectly labeled crates:

Crate:	First		Second		Third	
Incorrect Label:	"Potatoes"		"Sweet Potatoes"		"Potatoes & Sweet Potatoes"	
Possible Content:	sp	p&sp	p	p&sp	p	sp

The manager would have to simply *pick a veggie from the crate labeled "Potatoes & Sweet Potatoes,"* (the one called "third" in the table above). If the veggie he or she picked up is:

1. "*p*"—then because the label is known to be incorrect and yet the content includes potatoes, the correct label for this crate can only be

"Potatoes." Subsequently, the content of the second crate (incorrectly labeled "Sweet Potatoes"), must be "Potatoes & Sweet Potatoes" and thus, the label on the first one is "Sweet Potatoes."

2. "sp"—then because the label is known to be incorrect and yet the content includes sweet potatoes, the correct label for this crate can only be "Sweet Potatoes." Subsequently, the content of the first crate (incorrectly labeled "Potatoes"), must be "Potatoes & Sweet Potatoes" and thus, the label on the second one is "Potatoes."

In summary:

Manager Opens the Crate Labeled "Potatoes & Sweet Potatoes" and Picks a	First Crate Correct Label	Second Crate Correct Label	Third Crate Correct Label
Potato	"sp"	"p&sp"	"p"
Sweet Potato	"p&sp"	"p"	"sp"

Mind Game Solution 16

In 24 hours, the worm would advance 2 feet in his quest to get to the top. As a result, at the end of 25 days (and nights), it would advance 50 feet and thus be 5 feet away from the top. At the end of the next day (during day time, or before the night would set in), after advancing another 5 feet, the worm would finally reach the top of the well. The answer therefore is **26** days!

Mind Game Solution 17

It turns out that the solution is not unique. The following are examples (8) of markings that satisfy the requirements of the problem. Note that the probability that the sum of the outcomes is 1, 2, 3, 4, 5, 6, 7, 8, 9, 10, 11, or 12 is *always* 1 in 12.

For example, in the fourth row from the top (shaded),

- the probability of the sum to be "1" is equal to the probability of rolling a "1" (first die) and a "0" (second die), or $\frac{1}{2} \times \frac{1}{6} = \frac{1}{12}$

- the probability of the sum to be "9" is equal to the probability of rolling a "7" (first die) and a "2" (second die) or $\frac{1}{2} \times \frac{1}{6} = \frac{1}{12}$

In the example above, we only calculated two of the 12 possible outcomes—the ones resulting in a sum of 1 and 9. In addition, note that the left die—having only two numbers—will always contribute $\frac{1}{2}$ to the compound probability whereas the right die—being marked with 6 different numbers—will always contribute with a probability of $\frac{1}{6}$. Thus, the combined probability (the product) is always $\frac{1}{12}$.

First Die Markings						Second Die Markings					
1	1	1	2	2	2	0	2	4	6	8	10
1	1	1	3	3	3	0	1	4	5	8	9
1	1	1	4	4	4	0	1	2	6	7	8
1	1	1	7	7	7	0	1	2	3	4	5
0	0	0	1	1	1	1	3	5	7	9	11
0	0	0	2	2	2	1	2	5	6	9	10
0	0	0	3	3	3	1	2	3	7	8	9
0	0	0	6	6	6	1	2	3	4	5	6

Mind Game Solution 18

The problem can be solved in two steps, as follows:

1. light up—simultaneously—one string from both ends and the second string from one end only;
2. the first string will burn completely after 20/2 = 10 minutes (when the flames started at both ends would meet in the middle) at which point one lights up the other end of the second string on fire. From that moment on, the time needed for the second string to burn completely will be 10/2 = 5 minutes and that is exactly when 10 + 5 = **15 minutes** will have elapsed from the beginning of the experiment.

Mind Game Solution 19

The answers given to Avery by her three classmates were summarized below:

	Mary	John	Anna	Eric
Mary	-	2	1	3
John	1	-	2	3
Anna	2	3	-	1

One way to solve the problem is by analyzing the answers given by the students in the same order (i.e., Mary, John, and Anna, first, second, and third, respectively), assuming a correct answer and thus having to look at three different scenarios (given that only one in three answers can be considered true).

Assumption #1: Mary was right picking Eric at third or

	Mary	John	Anna	Eric
Mary	-	2 (false)	1 (false)	3 (true)
John	1 (valid)	-	2 (not valid)	3 (not valid)
Anna	2 (not valid)	3 (not valid)	-	1 (not valid)

or

	Mary	John	Anna	Eric
Mary	-	2 (false)	1 (false)	3 (true)
John	1 (not valid)	-	2 (valid)	3 (not valid)
Anna	2 (not valid)	3 (not valid)	-	1 (not valid)

Assumption #2: Mary was right picking John at second or

	Mary	John	Anna	Eric
Mary	-	2 (true)	1 (false)	3 (false)
John	1 (valid)	-	2 (not valid)	3 (not valid)
Anna	2 (not valid)	3 (not valid)	-	1 (not valid)

or

	Mary	John	Anna	Eric
Mary	-	2 (true)	1 (false)	3 (false)
John	1 (not valid)	-	2 (not valid)	3 (valid)
Anna	2 (not valid)	3 (not valid)	-	1 (not valid)

Assumption #3: Mary was right picking Anna at first or

	Mary	John	Anna	Eric
Mary	-	2 (false)	1 (true)	3 (false)
John	1 (not valid)	-	2 (not valid)	3 (valid)
Anna	2 (valid)	3 (not valid)	-	1 (not valid)

The only scenario that validated a correct answer for Anna is the one described in assumption #3. As a result, the correct outcome of the race was Anna, Mary, Eric, and John in the 1st, 2nd, 3rd, and 4th place, respectively.

Mind Game Solution 20

This is a classic word problem that can be easily translated into algebra by introducing two variables: W and B, denoting the number of white and black tokens that Jeremy removed from the box after the initial 13 tokens (6 white and 7 black) had been removed.

With these notations and given the fact that the least number of white tokens that would give Jeremy more white than black tokens (overall) would have to be equal with the number of black tokens plus one, one can write the following two equations:

1. $W + B = 17$
2. $6 + W = 7 + B + 1$

The second equation gives us $B = W - 2$ which substituted in the first equation results in

$$W + W - 2 = 17 \text{ or } W = 9.5$$

Given that the number of tokens must be a whole number, it follows that the least number of white tokens that—out of the 17 tokens—needed to be removed to give Jeremy more white than black tokens overall is **10**.

Mind Game Solution 21

	14	15	16	17	18	19	days/months
May		X	X			X	3
June				X	X		2
July	X		X				2
August	X	X		X			3
months/day	2	2	2	2	1	1	

Adam: When he says, "I don't know when your birthday is," of course he doesn't know, as for each month he has more than one option to choose from. When he says, "but I know Tom doesn't know either," we can conclude that the only way Tom (who knows the day) would have the answer was if the dates where either "18" or "19" in which case he would only have one option to choose from . . . thus now we know that the month cannot be May or June!

Tom: When he says, "I didn't know originally," looking at the table above, Tom would know the answer only if the dates were either "18" or "19" so, like in the previous case we rule those days out (this info is redundant). When he says, "but now I do," the new info that Tom now has is that the month is either July or August (see above). Because he now knows the answer, we infer that the day cannot be "14" as—in that case—he would have two options to choose from (July and August.) We conclude that the possible dates are July 16, August 15, or August 16. (Tom knows the day; we don't!)

Adam: When he says, "Well, now I know too!", he realized that the choice of days was narrowed down to "15," "16," and "17," but Adam couldn't be certain if the month was August (he'd have two options). But because "he now knows," we conclude that Maria's birthday is
                              July 16th.

Conclusion

As stated in the introduction, the novelty of this book primarily consists in a concentrated effort to emphasize *critical thinking/analytic skills* over memorization and trial and error. As a result, making this book part of the material used to prepare for the PSAT/SAT will add a holistic dimension to the study of math, making it a perfect companion for students entering college life—independent of the major of their choice.

In addition, the book comes with an online test that includes the math portion of a complete SAT and an analysis tool for test results assessment and recommendations. The latter is a novel and handy instrument that should help the students quantify the level of progress in achieving their desired level in their test preparation efforts.

Although an effort was made to provide a quick reference to most (if not all) PSAT/SAT math topics, the main value of the book is in its collection of 235 test problems (in addition to the 58 problems used for the online test) and 21 brain teasers/mind games to help students improve their reading comprehension and analytic/critical thinking skills. Most problems are solved as "test cases" and were selected primarily for being representative of genres/categories present in real tests and their suitability for showcasing the importance of reasoning, logic, and analytic skills.

A Final Word

I really hope you enjoyed and found this book useful. I want to hear from you so please feel free to send your comments to dan.celenti@gmail.com. I promise to do my best to respond and also to take your feedback into account for future editions or even new (and similar) projects.

—D.C.

Appendix A

Answer to the problem on pp. 11–12.

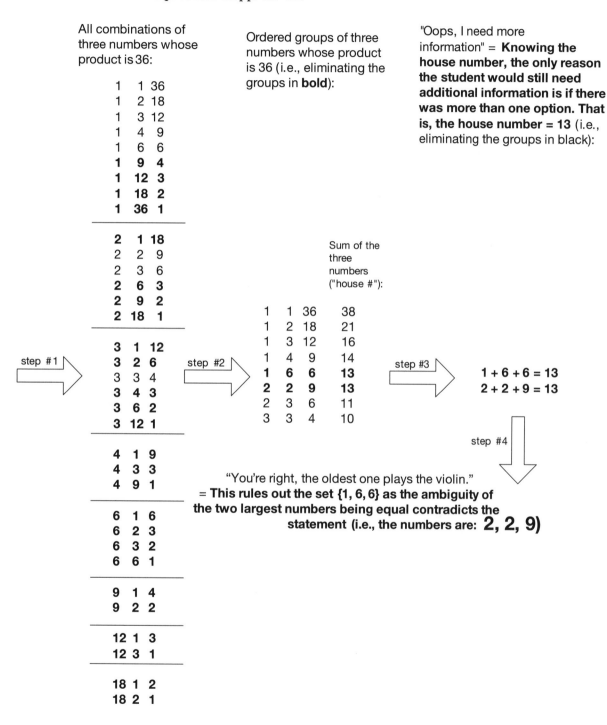

All combinations of three numbers whose product is 36:

Ordered groups of three numbers whose product is 36 (i.e., eliminating the groups in **bold**):

"Oops, I need more information" = **Knowing the house number, the only reason the student would still need additional information is if there was more than one option. That is, the house number = 13** (i.e., eliminating the groups in black):

Sum of the three numbers ("house #"):

step #1

step #2

step #3

step #4

1	1	36	38
1	2	18	21
1	3	12	16
1	4	9	14
1	**6**	**6**	**13**
2	**2**	**9**	**13**
2	3	6	11
3	3	4	10

1 + 6 + 6 = 13
2 + 2 + 9 = 13

"You're right, the oldest one plays the violin."
= **This rules out the set {1, 6, 6} as the ambiguity of the two largest numbers being equal contradicts the statement (i.e., the numbers are: 2, 2, 9)**

```
1   1  36
1   2  18
1   3  12
1   4   9
1   6   6
1   9   4
1  12   3
1  18   2
1  36   1
_____
2   1  18
2   2   9
2   3   6
2   6   3
2   9   2
2  18   1
_____
3   1  12
3   2   6
3   3   4
3   4   3
3   6   2
3  12   1
_____
4   1   9
4   3   3
4   9   1
_____
6   1   6
6   2   3
6   3   2
6   6   1
_____
9   1   4
9   2   2
_____
12  1   3
12  3   1
_____
18  1   2
18  2   1
```

Note that the very fact that the student needed "additional" information should predict that at least two sets of numbers satisfy the condition that their product (36) will add up to the number of his house.

303

Appendix B:
Solutions to On
Your Own Problems

Problem	1	2	3	4	5
Answer	"D" (46)	200	"D" (ae)	36	6400

Problem	6	7	8	9	10
Answer	36	3^k	128	27:1	10

Problem	11	12	13	14	15
Answer	122	$-\dfrac{b}{a}$	37	84°	2

Problem	16	17	18	19	20
Answer	(1,1)	128	34	95	8,13

Problem	21	22	23	24	25
Answer	$\dfrac{1}{7}$	$\dfrac{1}{2}$	C	C	5

References

College Board. (2015). *SAT percentile ranks for 2015 college-bound seniors*. Retrieved from https://secure-media.collegeboard.org/digitalServices/pdf/sat/sat-percentile-ranks-gender-ethnicity-2015.pdf

College Board. (2016). *Concordance tables*. Retrieved from https://collegereadiness.collegeboard.org/pdf/higher-ed-brief-sat-concordance.pdf

About the Author

Dan Celenti holds a Ph.D. in Applied Physics and has worked as a scientist, engineer, and educator (college professor and tutor). His wealth of experience—from conducting research in plasma physics and developing software for simulation of integrated circuits, to developing architectures for voice and data communication networks—has enabled him to take a pragmatic and holistic approach to the study of math.

Dan lives with his wife and their 16-year-old son in Holmdel, NJ. In his spare time—when he doesn't "do math" (an activity he prefers to refer to as "playing mind games")—he likes to play tennis, go skiing, play guitar, read, watch independent movies, coach Little League basketball, spend time in Manhattan, hang out with his friends, and travel the world: a world in which he truly believes that "math is in everything!"

Common Core State Standards Alignment

Grade Level	Common Core State Standards in Math
Grade 5	5.G.A Graph points on the coordinate plane to solve real-world and mathematical problems.
Grade 6	6.G.A Solve real-world and mathematical problems involving area, surface area, and volume.
	6.RP.A Understand ratio concepts and use ratio reasoning to solve problems.
	6.NS.A Apply and extend previous understandings of multiplication and division to divide fractions by fractions.
	6.NS.B Compute fluently with multi-digit numbers and find common factors and multiples.
	6.NS.C Apply and extend previous understandings of numbers to the system of rational numbers.
	6.EE.A Apply and extend previous understandings of arithmetic to algebraic expressions.
	6.EE.B Reason about and solve one-variable equations and inequalities.
	6.EE.C Represent and analyze quantitative relationships between dependent and independent variables.
	6.SP.A Develop understanding of statistical variability.
	6.SP.B Summarize and describe distributions.

Grade Level	Common Core State Standards in Math
Grade 7	7.G.A Draw construct, and describe geometrical figures and describe the relationships between them.
	7.G.B Solve real-life and mathematical problems involving angle measure, area, surface area, and volume.
	7.RP.A Analyze proportional relationships and use them to solve real-world and mathematical problems.
	7.NS.A Apply and extend previous understandings of operations with fractions.
	7.EE.A Use properties of operations to generate equivalent expressions.
	7.EE.B Solve real-life and mathematical problems using numerical and algebraic expressions and equations.
	7.SP.A Use random sampling to draw inferences about a population.
	7.SP.B Draw informal comparative inferences about two populations.
	7.SP.C Investigate chance processes and develop, use, and evaluate probability models.
Grade 8	8.G.B Understand and apply the Pythagorean Theorem.
	8.NS.A Know that there are numbers that are not rational, and approximate them by rational numbers.
	8.EE.A Work with radicals and integer exponents.
	8.EE.B Understand the connections between proportional relationships, lines, and linear equations.
	8.EE.C Analyze and solve linear equations and pairs of simultaneous linear equations.
	8.F.A Define, evaluate, and compare functions.
	8.F.B Use functions to model relationships between quantities.
High School Number & Quantity	HSN-RN.A Extend the properties of exponents to rational exponents.
	HSN-Q.A Reason quantitatively and use units to solve problems.
HS Algebra	HSA-SSE.A Interpret the structure of expressions.
	HSA-SSE.B Write expressions in equivalent forms to solve problems.
	HSA-APR.A Perform arithmetic operations on polynomials.
	HSA-APR.B Understand the relationship between zeros and factors of polynomials.
	HSA-APR.C Use polynomial identities to solve problems.
	HSA-APR.D Rewrite rational expressions.
	HSA-CED.A Create equations that describe numbers or relationships.
	HSA-REI.A Understand solving equations as a process of reasoning and explain the reasoning.

Grade Level	Common Core State Standards in Math
HS Algebra, *continued*	HSA-REI.B Solve equations and inequalities in one variable.
	HSA-REI.C Solve systems of equations.
	HSA-REI.D Represent and solve equations and inequalities graphically.
HS Functions	HSF-IF.A Understand the concept of a function and use function notation.
	HSF-IF.B Interpret functions that arise in applications in terms of the context.
	HSF-BF.A Build a function that models a relationship between two quantities.
	HSF-BF.B Build new functions from existing functions.
HS Geometry	HSG-C.A Understand and apply theorems about circles.
	HSG-C.B Find arc lengths and areas of sectors of circles.
	HSG-GPE.B Use coordinates to prove simple geometric theorems algebraically.
HS Statistics & Probability	HSS-ID.A Summarize, represent, and interpret data on a single count or measurement variable.
	HSS-CP.A Understand independence and conditional probability and use them to interpret data.
	HSS-CP.B Use the rules of probability to compute probabilities of compound events.
	HSS-MD.A Calculate expected values and use them to solve problems.
	HSS-MD.B Use probability to evaluate outcomes of decisions.

Key for Grades 5–8: G = Geometry; RP = Ratios & Proportional Relationships; NS = The Number System; EE = Expressions & Equations; F = Functions; SP = Statistics & Probability